W9-BFV-424

Science Concepts SECOND SERIES

Plate Tectonics

Revised Edition

Alvin Silverstein, Virginia Silverstein,
and Laura Silverstein Nunn

 Twenty-First Century Books
Minneapolis

Text copyright © 2009 by Alvin Silverstein, Virginia Silverstein, and Laura Silverstein Nunn

All rights reserved. International copyright secured. No part of this book may be reproduced, stored in a retrieval system, or transmitted in any form or by any means—electronic, mechanical, photocopying, recording, or otherwise—without the prior written permission of Lerner Publishing Group, Inc., except for the inclusion of brief quotations in an acknowledged review.

Twenty-First Century Books
A division of Lerner Publishing Group, Inc.
241 First Avenue North
Minneapolis, MN 55401 U.S.A.

Website address: www.lernerbooks.com

Library of Congress Cataloging-in-Publication Data

Silverstein, Alvin.
    Plate tectonics / by Alvin & Virginia Silverstein & Laura Silverstein Nunn. — Rev. ed.
        p.   cm. — (Science concepts. Second series)
    Includes bibliographical references and index.
    ISBN 978–0–7613–3936–6 (lib. bdg. : alk. paper)
    1. Plate tectonics—Juvenile literature. I. Silverstein, Virginia B. II. Nunn, Laura Silverstein. III. Title.
    QE511.4.S55 2009
    551.1'36—dc22   2007051039

Manufactured in the United States of America
1 2 3 4 5 6 – DP – 14 13 12 11 10 09

Contents

chapter one

Our Planet Earth

We usually think of the ground under our feet as firm and solid, but it is not always so. During an earthquake, the ground trembles and shakes. The most violent earthquakes can send huge buildings crashing down and crumple bridges and superhighways. When a volcano erupts, a quiet mountain begins to rumble and smoke and then literally blows its top. A cloud of hot ash spews out, and burning hot lava—melted rock—pours down the mountainside, destroying everything in its path.

Much slower changes also occur on our not-so-quiet planet Earth. Huge mountain ranges thrust up in places where only flatlands or even sea bottoms existed. Other mountains are gradually wearing away.

Early humans wondered about their world and its mysteries. What enormous forces could make the solid ground shake and even split apart? What could make a peaceful mountain turn into an erupting

Hindus in ancient India believed that Earth was carried on the backs of four elephants, which stood on the shell of a turtle.

volcano? People made up myths, or stories, to explain the workings of the world. The ancient Romans, for example, thought a volcanic mountain was the workshop of the fire god Vulcan. Hindus in ancient India believed that Earth was as flat as a dinner plate. They thought it rested on the backs of four elephants standing on the shell of a giant turtle. If the animals moved, they caused an earthquake.

In the twentieth century, a scientific theory was finally worked out to explain earthquakes, volcanoes, and many other mysteries of our planet. This is the plate tectonic theory. To understand it, we first need to learn a few things about our planet Earth.

An ancient Greek conception of the universe is depicted in an engraving made in Amsterdam, the Netherlands, in 1660.

Earth: The Inside Story

By the sixth century B.C., Greek scientists had figured out that Earth was round, like a ball. They thought, however, that it was a solid ball located at the center of the universe.

Beginning in the late fifteenth century, as explorers discovered more of the world, they were impressed with the huge oceans. They wondered where all the water had come from. They thought perhaps the solid part of our planet was just an outer crust, covering an inside filled with water. Erupting volcanoes, however, suggested that Earth contained fiery-hot melted rock inside.

By the late 1800s, most geologists (scientists who study Earth) agreed on the following: Our planet most likely has a solid inner core made of heavy metals, an outer crust of rock, and hot melted rock in between. The liquid part, called the mantle, is kept constantly churning by currents produced by the heat of the core. At times, some of the mantle material bursts out through weak spots in the crust, such as when a volcano erupts.

How Do We Know Earth Is Round?

People in modern times have no problem believing our planet is round. We've seen pictures of it, sent back by orbiting spacecraft. The ancient Greeks had no way of looking at Earth from the outside. So they had to depend on clues. Ships sailing away at sea seemed to sink as they reached the horizon. Eventually only the tops of their sails were visible, and soon even those disappeared. Travelers told how new stars appeared in the sky as they sailed north. Meanwhile, the familiar ones in the south dropped out of sight. The Greek philosopher and scientist Aristotle pointed out another piece of evidence: during a lunar eclipse, when Earth comes between the Sun and Moon, Earth casts a round shadow on the Moon.

This total lunar eclipse was seen from Australia in August 2007. A lunar eclipse is when Earth comes between the Sun and Moon. The next total lunar eclipse will occur in 2011.

Scientists studying earthquakes later found evidence supporting these ideas about Earth's structure. An instrument called a seismograph, developed in 1880, measures the waves of energy transmitted through the planet during a quake. Like light rays passing from air through a glass of water, the seismic waves of an earthquake bend slightly as they go from one material to another. The seismograph records show a bend about 20 to 50 miles (32 to 80 kilometers) down from Earth's surface. This marks the boundary between the solid crust and the mantle. Another bend much farther down toward the planet's center marks the boundary between the mantle and the core.

A seismologist in the Philippines points out earthquake activity on a seismograph.

You can think of Earth as something like a giant piece of fruit. Its inner core is like the pit of a cherry or peach. The mantle is like the layer of juicy pulp in the middle of the fruit. The crust is like the outer skin of the fruit. Compared to the size of the whole earth, the crust is a rather thin skin. In fact, if you made a scale model of Earth the size of a melon, its skin would be thinner than a hair. You would need a magnifying glass to see any of its details. Even the peak of Mount Everest, the highest mountain, would be too small to see.

The crust, the outermost layer, is not the same thickness all over Earth's surface. Under the oceans, it is rather thin, in some places less than 4 miles (6 km) thick. The continents (the landmasses) are formed by thicker parts of the crust. Some areas are about 16 miles (25 km) thick. Others, such as those under the plains and deserts, are about 20 to 25 miles (30 to 40 km) thick. Earth's crust is as thick as 62 miles (100 km) under the highest mountain ranges. Even the "thin" parts of the crust are not very thin compared to the distances we usually deal with. For example, the deepest mine in the world is less than 2.5 miles (4 km) deep, and the deepest holes ever drilled went down about 9 miles (15 km).

The mantle, Earth's middle layer, extends almost to the surface. It is about 1,800 miles (2,900 km) thick and is made of various rocky materials. The mantle is actually solid, but

Earth's Layers

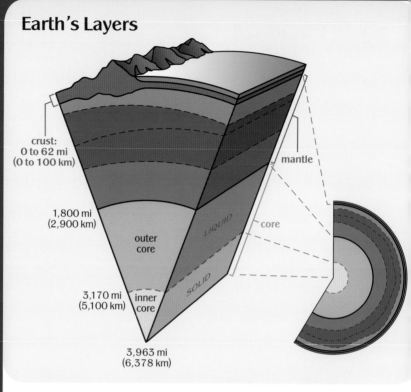

crust:
0 to 62 mi
(0 to 100 km)

mantle

1,800 mi
(2,900 km)

LIQUID

core

outer
core

SOLID

3,170 mi
(5,100 km)

inner
core

3,963 mi
(6,378 km)

Earth's inside is a series of layers. The inner core, at the center, is a dense ball of solid iron and nickel. The outer core is hot molten iron, mixed with other elements. The lower mantle is solid rock but can flow under pressure. The upper mantle is hot molten rock. The thin outer layer is Earth's solid, rocky crust. (This diagram is not drawn to scale. The crust is really much thinner, compared to the other layers.)

under slow, gradual pressure, it can flow like a thick liquid. (Think of mud.) The pressure is highest in the lower mantle. Rocks that float down from the upper mantle are compressed (squashed) under the higher pressure and become very dense. In the upper mantle, hot rocks melt into a liquid called magma.

Earth's core—the innermost part—actually consists of two separate layers. The inner core is a solid ball of iron and nickel, about 1,500 miles (2,400 km) in diameter. It is very dense and is under enormous pressure—3.6 million times the pressure at the surface of the crust. The inner core is also extremely hot—more than 10,000°F (6,000°C). That's as hot as the surface of the sun! A liquid outer core surrounds the inner core. It is believed to be made up of mostly molten iron, with small amounts of other elements, such as silicon, sulfur, and oxygen. This hot liquid part of the core is about 1,400 miles (2,250 km) thick.

Moving Parts

Earth's rocky crust, together with a layer of hard mantle just beneath it, is broken up into a dozen large pieces and some smaller ones. These pieces are called tectonic plates. (*Tecton* is the Greek word for "builder.") They fit together like the pieces of a jigsaw puzzle. The tectonic plates are about 30 to 50 miles (50 to 80 km) thick. Some of them are huge in comparison to others. For example, the whole North American continent rests on a single large plate. This North American Plate also includes parts of the surrounding oceans and extends all the way to Iceland. The distance across the plate from

> ### Did You Know?
> Earth's tectonic plates move at about the same rate as your fingernails grow—an average of a little more than one inch (2.5 centimeters) per year.

California to Iceland is about 6,200 miles (10,000 km). A little plate that fits next to it, the Juan de Fuca Plate off the coast of Washington State, is just 310 miles (500 km) wide. (For a map of the tectonic plates, see below.)

Earth's tectonic plates float on the mantle. Flowing movements in the mantle cause the plates to move about, sometimes pulling apart, crashing into one another, or rubbing sideways along their edges. This is a very slow process. The plates move between 0.5 inch and 4 inches (1 and 10 cm) per year. But they are so massive that even these slow, creeping

Earth's tectonic plates fit together like the pieces of a giant, 3-D jigsaw puzzle. The plates float on the mantle and move slowly, sliding together, apart, or alongside one another. Arrows show the directions the plates are moving.

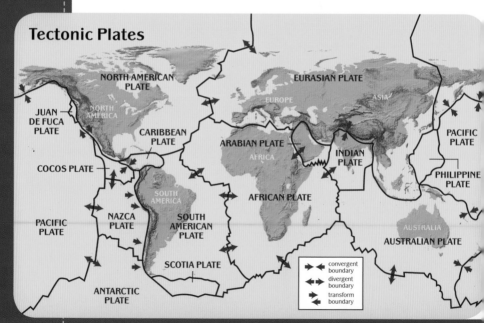

Tectonic Plates

NORTH AMERICAN PLATE

EURASIAN PLATE

EUROPE

ASIA

JUAN DE FUCA PLATE

NORTH AMERICA

CARIBBEAN PLATE

ARABIAN PLATE

INDIAN PLATE

PACIFIC PLATE

COCOS PLATE

AFRICA

PHILIPPINE PLATE

PACIFIC PLATE

NAZCA PLATE

SOUTH AMERICA

SOUTH AMERICAN PLATE

AFRICAN PLATE

AUSTRALIA

AUSTRALIAN PLATE

SCOTIA PLATE

convergent boundary
divergent boundary
transform boundary

ANTARCTIC PLATE

This deep crack in Earth's crust, near Mammoth Lakes in California, is from earthquake activity where two tectonic plates meet.

movements can cause tremendous effects. Earthquakes may occur at the edges of the moving plates that collide. Volcanoes can form where two plates move apart. And the edges of bumping plates may buckle and fold, building up mountain ranges. The discovery of all this was a long process, filled with errors along the way.

chapter two

Discovering Plate Tectonics

Early explorers of the world drew maps of the lands they visited. These early maps were rough and often inaccurate. Nonetheless, they were detailed enough to show that the various continents seemed to fit together like pieces of a jigsaw puzzle. For example, the bulge on the east coast of South America appeared to fit nicely into a notch on the west coast of Africa. The Dutch mapmaker Abraham Ortelius was one of the first to notice this. In 1596 he commented about the fit of the coastlines in his book on geography. He suggested that the American continents had been "torn away from Europe and Africa . . . by earthquakes and floods."

The English philosopher Francis Bacon wrote in 1620 that the fit between the coastlines of the continents on opposite sides of the Atlantic Ocean could not be just an accident. However, he had no suggestions on what could have caused it.

In 1750 the French naturalist Georges de Buffon wrote about the way South America and Africa fit together. He proposed that perhaps at one time, in the distant past, these two lands were joined together. In 1858 the French geographer Antonio Snider-Pellegrini actually drew "before" and "after" maps showing how the American continents had once been joined to Europe and Africa. By that time, other kinds of evidence began to support his idea.

Pieces of the Puzzle

In the early nineteenth century, the German explorer Alexander von Humboldt reported that the rocks of Brazil, on the east coast of South America, were quite similar to those of the Congo, in western Africa. Humboldt suggested that these lands were originally joined until a huge tidal wave carved out the Atlantic Ocean. More clues to the great "Earth puzzle" were provided by naturalists who traveled between the continents. They reported that the same species of turtles, snakes, and lizards could be found in both South America and Africa. They also found similar fossils, preserved remains

Fossils of this freshwater reptile have been found only in parts of Africa and South America.

of ancient life. Visiting naturalists also discovered many similarities between plant and animal species in Europe and North America. For example, fossils of camels were found in both North and South America, even though present-day camels live only in Africa. Some scientists wondered if land bridges once connected all the continents, but such bridges later sank into the seas.

Scientists offered many different theories to explain how Earth's continents formed. Some thought that sudden great catastrophes had broken apart landmasses and formed the oceans. An example would be the great flood described in the Bible and in the myths of people elsewhere. Other scientists thought Earth's lands had gone through a series of slower, more gradual changes. Modern scientists believe that both catastrophes and slow, gradual processes have helped to shape the surface of our planet.

In 1885 Eduard Suess, an Austrian geologist, published a work called *The Face of the Earth*. In it he suggested that in the distant past (about 180 million years ago), the continents were condensed into two giant landmasses: a southern area he called Gondwanaland and a northern one he named Laurasia. According to Suess's theory, Laurasia ultimately separated into Europe, Asia, and North America, while Gondwanaland gave rise to the rest of the continents.

In 1908 two U.S. geologists, Frank Taylor and Howard Baker, independently suggested that the continents had moved in the past. Taylor thought, for

A Lost Continent?

In the 300s B.C., the Greek philosopher Plato wrote about an ancient island in the west, Atlantis. Atlantians were rich and powerful and had a brilliant civilization. But they became so greedy and corrupt that the gods punished them. In a single day and night, huge explosions shook the island and Atlantis sank into the Atlantic Ocean.

The story of Atlantis may have been just a myth, or a fable. Plato made up to illustrate his philosophical ideas. For many centuries, though, Europeans wondered about "lost Atlantis" and sent out expeditions to look for it. The catastrophe theories of the late eighteenth and nineteenth centuries provided new fuel for believers in Atlantis. They thought Atlantis was the part of Gondwanaland that sank when the Atlantic Ocean was formed.

example, that the mountain ranges in Europe and Asia formed from the movement of the continents toward the equator. But since neither could offer any evidence to support their theory, they were not taken seriously.

The Father of Continental Drift

Alfred Wegener, a German meteorologist, made important contributions to weather science. He was the first to use

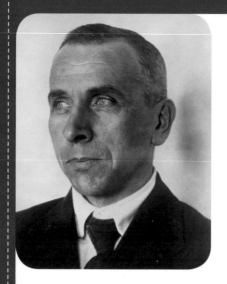

German meteorologist Alfred Wegener is known as the father of continental drift. This theory explains how the continents are slowly drifting around Earth.

balloons to track air currents, for example. But he is remembered most for the theory of continental drift. In 1911 Wegener happened to read a scientific paper on the fossils of identical plants and animals that had been found in lands on opposite sides of the Atlantic Ocean. Instead of accepting the existing theory—that the continents had once been connected by land bridges—Wegener focused on the close fit between the coastlines of Africa and South America. He began to look for evidence that these continents had once been joined. For example, the layers of rocks in South Africa matched those of Brazil. Mountain ranges seemed to begin on one continent and continue on another, although separated by thousands of miles. The Appalachian Mountains in North America, for instance, matched up neatly with the Highlands of Scotland. "It is just as if we were to refit the torn pieces of a newspaper by their matching edges," Wegener wrote.

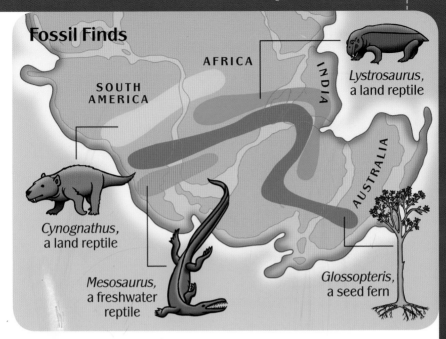

Fossil Finds

AFRICA

SOUTH AMERICA

INDIA

Lystrosaurus, a land reptile

AUSTRALIA

Cynognathus, a land reptile

Mesosaurus, a freshwater reptile

Glossopteris, a seed fern

Locations of fossil remains of ancient plants and animals suggest the continents were once connected.

Another intriguing fact was that fossils in various places often showed that the climate in those regions had been quite different in the past. For example, fossils of tropical plants had been found in Spitsbergen, an island in the cold Arctic Ocean that must once have been warm. Rock deposits from glaciers were present in India, Australia, Africa, and South America, suggesting that these warm areas must once have been in a cold climate, perhaps near the South Pole.

Wegener said that these findings could be explained if all the landmasses on Earth had once been joined together. He suggested that about 300 million years ago, they were parts of a huge supercontinent. He called it Pangaea (from Greek words meaning "all the earth"). This supercontinent broke apart, like a cracked sheet of ice, and the pieces (modern-day

Continental Drift

200 million years ago

150 million years ago

100 million years ago

50 million years ago

Alfred Wegener proposed that Earth's continents had once been joined as a single landmass, which he called Pangaea. This landmass gradually broke into pieces over many millions of years.

continents) have been slowly drifting away from one another ever since. Wegener first presented his theory in a lecture in 1912 and then in a book, *The Origin of Continents and Oceans,* in 1915.

Geologists of the time called the idea of continental drift "ludicrous." Wegener thought that the continents moved through Earth's crust like icebreakers plowing through ice sheets. Other scientists asked how the soft, light rocks of the continents could break through the hard, dense rocks of the ocean floor. And where did the energy to push the continents apart come from? Wegener thought that Earth's rotation on its axis, along with the gravitational pull of the Sun and the Moon, provided the energy for the movement. But these forces were too weak. One scientist calculated that a tidal force strong enough to move continents would stop Earth's rotation within less than a year! When Wegener died in 1930 at the age of fifty, most scientists still thought his theory was ridiculous.

Under the Surface

Not everyone rejected Alfred Wegener's theory. Arthur Holmes, a British geologist, thought the continental drift idea seemed reasonable. In 1929 Holmes suggested that the landmasses at the surface might be moving because of convection currents in the mantle beneath them. Scientists of the time did not pay much attention to this suggestion. But most modern scientists do believe that convection in the mantle plays an important role in the movements in Earth's crust.

In the late 1930s, David Griggs, a U.S. geologist, showed that at very high temperatures and pressures, seemingly solid rock actually flows slowly. Researchers who explored the ocean bottom in the 1940s found that there wasn't as much sediment (solid matter that had settled to the bottom) on some parts of the ocean floor as there should have been if it were as old as the landmasses. And the oldest rocks that were found in the sea were about 200 million years old—much younger than the rocks on land.

What Is Convection?

When a pot of soup boils, the liquid begins to bubble and churn. Pieces of vegetables, meat, and other solid particles rise to the surface and then disappear back into the boiling soup. The heat from the burners under the pot provides the energy for this movement. The heated soup near the bottom rises. But then it gradually cools as it gets farther from the heat source. Eventually it falls and is replaced by new heated material. The circular flows of matter in a heated liquid are called convection currents. These convection currents help spread the heat throughout the entire pot of soup. The same thing happens when a radiator heats up a whole room. Convection currents in the air help to spread the heat around the room. Convection currents in the atmosphere create winds.

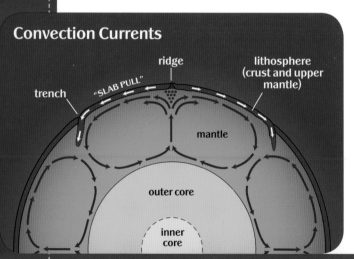

Convection Currents

trench · "SLAB PULL" · ridge · lithosphere (crust and upper mantle) · mantle · outer core · inner core

Convection currents in the mantle most likely play an important role in the movements of Earth's crust.

The explorers also found that the outlines of the continental shelves (the relatively shallow-water areas just off the coast) fit together even better than the outlines of the landmasses themselves.

Rock layers like these in the Swiss Alps were used as evidence that mountains could be formed by continents colliding.

Meanwhile, Emile Argand, a Swiss geologist, argued that the folded, buckled pattern of the rock layers in the Swiss Alps could best be explained if the mountains had been formed in a collision of continents. The South African geologist Alexander Du Toit, another firm believer in Wegener's theory, spent his life accumulating evidence to support the concept of continental drift.

For three decades after Wegener's death, evidence supporting his theory gradually built up. Wegener's supporters were just a small, scattered minority, though. The majority of scientists were still unconvinced. As one geologist remarked at a 1928 meeting of the American Association of Petroleum Geologists, "If we are to believe Wegener's hypothesis, we must forget everything which has been learned in the last seventy years and start all over again."

chapter three

Studies in the 1950s revealed some surprising new information about our planet—evidence that would support Wegener's continental drift concept. Some of that information came from the study of Earth's natural magnetism.

Earth Is a Magnet

In the sixteenth century, the English scientist William Gilbert correctly guessed that Earth acts like a huge magnet. That is why a compass needle always points to the North Pole. Gilbert could not explain how this happened. Today we know that the magnetism is created by the flow of molten iron and nickel in the outer part of Earth's core. These metals are naturally magnetic. Their movements generate electric currents, which in turn produce a magnetic field. Earth's magnetic field extends not only through the planet but also about 37,000 miles (60,000 km) out into space.

If a bar of magnetic metal hanging from a thread is allowed to move freely, it will move so that one end points toward the North Pole (in the Arctic region) and the other end points toward the South Pole (in the Antarctic region). This is basically how a compass works. The same thing happens to bits of metal in the rocks that form when molten lava from a volcano cools and solidifies. These rocks are like compasses, showing the location of north and south.

When geologists examined older layers of rocks, however, they made a curious discovery. The magnets in those rocks did not point exactly toward the North Pole. It seemed the more ancient the rocks, the farther they were from "true north." By comparing the way rocks from different time periods lined up, scientists in Europe found that about 250 million years ago, the magnetic North Pole was apparently located in Hawaii. Later, it wandered over to Japan, and finally it reached its present

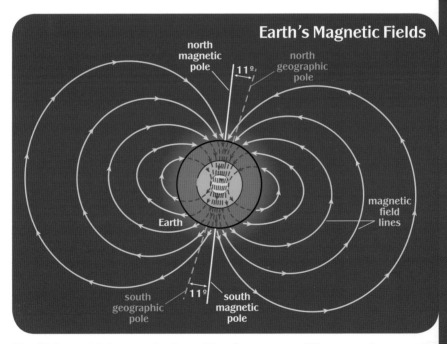

Earth's Magnetic Fields

north magnetic pole

11°

north geographic pole

magnetic field lines

Earth

south geographic pole

11°

south magnetic pole

Earth's iron-nickel core makes it act like a huge magnet. The magnetic field around it affects everything on the planet's surface and even for some distance out in space.

position in the Arctic. Observations of magnetic rocks in other continents also suggested that the North Pole had wandered over the ages. In each case, though, it seemed to have traveled over a different path, from various other locations to its present place. How could the North Pole have been located in different places at the same time? That was impossible.

What if the North Pole had actually stayed in the same place, but the continents had moved instead? Geologists took another look at Wegener's continental drift theory. If the continents had been moving apart after splitting off from a big supercontinent, the way the magnetic rocks were lined up would have changed over time. When the geologists figured out the positions of the moving continents at the time the magnetic rocks were formed, sure enough—the magnets in the rocks all pointed to the same North Pole.

Deep-Sea Story

The famous undersea explorer Jacques Cousteau first became fascinated with the ocean as an officer in the French navy during World War II (1939–1945). After the war was over, Cousteau helped develop scuba diving equipment and began to explore the ocean bottom along the continental shelf.

Cousteau and other divers discovered a lot of intriguing new information about the ocean basins during the 1950s and 1960s. They found that the ocean bottoms do not form smooth bowls, like a washbasin. They are just as varied as the continents, with huge underwater mountains, valleys, and canyons. A long mountain range, the Mid-Atlantic Ridge, was found in the middle of the Atlantic Ocean floor. Later, it was discovered that similar mountain ranges exist in all the ocean bottoms. They form an underwater ridge about 37,000 miles (60,000 km) long, winding around through the water-covered parts of the planet like the seam on a baseball.

A deep canyon, or trench, runs down the middle of each midocean ridge. These underwater mountain ranges are often shaken by earthquakes and volcanic eruptions. The trenches mark cracks in Earth's crust, where magma wells up from the mantle below and flows out continually as lava.

This trench in Thingvellir, Iceland, is part of the Mid-Atlantic Ridge. In the north, the ridge forms the boundary between the North American and Eurasian tectonic plates. Iceland is one of the few places where the Mid-Atlantic Ridge can be seen above sea level.

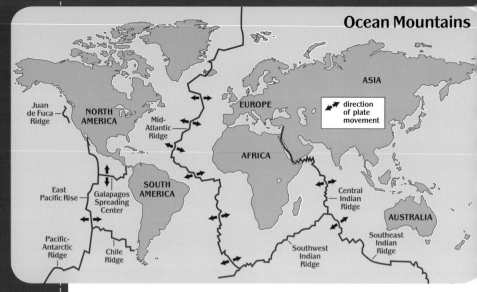

The Mid–Atlantic Ridge and other chains of underwater mountains under the world's oceans mark the boundaries of moving tectonic plates.

Deep trenches also occur in various parts of the ocean floor, dropping sharply to depths 5 to 6 miles (8 to 10 km) below the ocean surface. These trenches form a ring around the Pacific Ocean, along the western coasts of Central and South America, and in the midocean in the southwestern Pacific. There are trenches in the Indian Ocean too and even a few small ones in the Atlantic. These trenches are areas of frequent earthquake activity.

In 1959 U.S. geologist Harry Hess proposed a theory that he called seafloor spreading to account for these features of the ocean basins. He suggested that as the hot molten rock in the mantle slowly rises, it presses against the rock formations in the crust. When it reaches a weak spot, cracks form.

Creatures of the Deep

Most ocean plants and animals live near the ocean's surface, where they depend on the sun's energy for survival. Sunlight cannot reach the deep ocean waters, so temperatures are usually too cold—about 36°F (2°C)—to support life. But scientists have discovered that a whole community of life survives very well around gaps in the ocean floor called hydrothermal vents. Hydrothermal vents are underwater hot springs. They are often found near underwater volcanoes.

When a hydrothermal vent erupts, it spews superheated water—as high as 700°F (371°C)—that kills every living thing nearby. Soon, as the area cools to below 212°F (100°C), new life appears around the vents. Heat is a form of energy. Bacteria living in the deep sea can use this energy and sulfur compounds in the water to make food. They gather around the vents and multiply. The bacteria, in turn, become food for sea animals such as crabs, tube worms, and mussels, which also gather around the vents. In just one year, the number of species living around a vent can double.

Hydrothermal tube worms thrive deep on the ocean bottom.

Did You Know?

The deepest place in the world is in the Mariana Trench in the North Pacific Ocean. It dips about 36,200 feet (11,033 meters) below sea level. Compare that with the world's highest land mountain, Mount Everest in Asia, whose peak is only 29,035 feet (8,850 m) above sea level. If Mount Everest were placed in the Mariana Trench, the mountain would be covered by more than one mile (1.6 km) of water!

The increased pressure causes the cracks to widen, allowing the hot magma to squeeze through. Finally, it breaks through to the ocean floor as molten lava. In contact with the cold ocean water, the lava cools down and forms hard rock. Each successive flow adds another layer, slowly building up ridges on the ocean floor. The upwelling material forces the ridge edges apart, and the seafloor slowly spreads.

If new material is continually being added to Earth's crust at the midocean ridges, is our planet getting larger? No, because older parts of the seafloor are continually being pushed down into the mantle at the deep trenches. So there is a kind of recycling process between Earth's crust and the mantle: old crust is melted down, and new crust forms when magma breaks through to the surface and solidifies.

Hess's theory of seafloor spreading provided what Wegener lacked: an explanation of *how* the continents could move through Earth's crust. In 1967 W. Jason Morgan, a U.S. geologist, and Dan McKenzie, a

This aerial view of Mount Everest in the Himalayas shows the highest land mountain on Earth.

British geologist, took the reasoning a step further. Each one independently suggested that Earth's surface is made up of a number of movable plates. In 1968 U.S. geologists Bryan L. Isacks, Jack E. Oliver, and Lynn R. Sykes suggested that these solid plates can move because they float on the liquid mantle beneath them. Thus, the plate tectonic theory was complete.

chapter four

Plate Tectonics in Action

Much of what scientists have learned about the ocean bottom came from the voyages of a single ship, the *Glomar Challenger*. From 1968 to 1983, this ship sailed the world's oceans, as well as the Mediterranean and Red seas. During these years, the *Challenger* drilled more than nineteen thousand core samples from 624 sites on the sea bottom. These rock samples, each 30 feet (9 m) long and 2.5 inches (6 cm) in diameter, provided a wealth of knowledge about Earth's crust and its history.

Since then other ships have continued to explore the ocean bottoms. The samples they have brought back have provided more information on the age of the ocean floor. Studies of the magnetic rocks from the ocean bottom have allowed scientists to calculate just how fast the seafloor was spreading (and how fast the continents were moving) at various times in the past.

Meanwhile, the use of satellites orbiting Earth has made it possible to measure exactly how fast

The **Glomar Challenger** *was the first research vessel specifically designed to drill into and take core samples out of the deep ocean floor.*

the continents are moving. The twenty-one satellites of the Global Positioning System (GPS), for example, continuously transmit radio signals back to Earth. Each GPS station on the ground compares signals from at least four satellites to determine its exact position relative to the other ground sites. From those data, its exact latitude, longitude, and elevation can be determined.

The results obtained in the past few decades have shown, among other things, that the North Atlantic Ocean formed about 189 million years ago. Eurasia and North America are moving apart at about 1 inch (2.5

Did You Know?

Scientists studying samples of magnetic rocks from the ocean bottom have determined that Earth's poles have reversed themselves every three million years or so. The North Pole was once in Antarctica—and it will be there again some time in the future!

cm) a year. The fastest-moving place in the world is a region in the South Pacific near Easter Island, known as the East Pacific Rise. It is traveling more than 6 inches (15 cm) each year.

How Plate Tectonics Works

Geologists have mapped the regions of volcanic and earthquake activity and seafloor spreading. They have found that these regions form a network of cracks over Earth's surface. This network outlines the irregular shapes of the plates that form Earth's crust. Actually, the plates also include the uppermost part of the mantle, which is cooler and harder than the rest of the mantle below it. Together the crust and uppermost mantle form the lithosphere (from the Greek *lithos*, meaning "stone"). It is a hard layer of rock, but—like an eggshell—it is brittle and can crack. The plates that form the lithosphere float on a hot, semisolid layer of mantle called the asthenosphere (from *asthenes*, the Greek word for "weak"). This part of the mantle can soften and flow under the action of high temperatures from below and the weight of the lithosphere above it. The flow of the asthenosphere allows the plates floating on it to move. This is a very slow process, occurring over long periods of time.

The lithosphere averages about 50 miles (80 km) thick. But certain parts are thicker than others. For example, the parts under the oceans are much thinner than those that form the continents—less

The Lithosphere

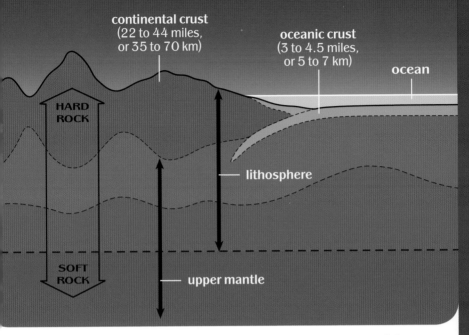

continental crust
(22 to 44 miles,
or 35 to 70 km)

oceanic crust
(3 to 4.5 miles,
or 5 to 7 km)

ocean

HARD
ROCK

lithosphere

SOFT
ROCK

upper mantle

Earth's tectonic plates include the crust and the uppermost part of the mantle.

than 9 miles (15 km) for the youngest parts of the seafloor to about 125 miles (200 km) or more in mountainous parts of the continents. Why don't the thick continental plates sink into the softer asthenosphere? The reason is that they are made of much lighter rocks than the denser lithosphere under the oceans.

The edges of tectonic plates are called plate boundaries. Scientists describe three main types of plate boundaries:

- *Divergent boundaries*, where the plates are moving away from one another and new crust is formed from the mantle material
- *Convergent boundaries*, where plates moving toward one another collide. The edge of one plate may dip under the

edge of the other. Crust is destroyed, melting down into mantle material.

- *Transform boundaries*, where plates are sliding past one another. No crust is destroyed, and no new crust is formed.

The plate movements at these boundaries produce quite different effects. These effects depend on what kind of plates are involved.

At divergent boundaries, magma rises to the surface. The plates pull apart, like two giant conveyer belts moving in opposite directions. As the hot molten rock cools, it hardens to form new crust at their edges.

Most of the divergent boundaries are found under the oceans. Magma oozes out slowly along the crack between the two plates. As new crust forms, the seafloor spreads and the ocean gets wider. The Mid-Atlantic Ridge is the best known example of this type. It is an underwater mountain range that circles the planet. Over the past 200 million years, the diverging plates formed the Atlantic Ocean.

In some areas along a divergent boundary, the oozing magma may be concentrated in one spot. Instead of spreading the seafloor, it builds up to form a volcanic island.

At convergent boundaries, plates move toward one another. When an oceanic plate collides with a continental plate, the thinner, denser oceanic plate may slip underneath the edge of the continental plate. Its greater weight pulls it down into the mantle.

Lava spurts through rifts in the ground surrounding Iceland's Krafla volcano, shown here in 1981.

Living Laboratory

The Mid-Atlantic Ridge runs through Iceland, which lies at the boundary of the North American and Eurasian plates. This northern island country is thus a kind of natural "laboratory," where scientists can study changes on land similar to those that occur deep under the sea. Iceland has a number of active volcanoes, with cracks in the ground around them. Near one of these volcanoes, Krafla, new cracks appear every so often, and those already present widen farther. Between 1975 and 1984, rifting (cracking) was so active that scientists call the decade the Krafla fissure swarm. During those ten years, the ground shifted about 23 feet (7 m).

Sometimes the rifting is combined with volcanic activity. Just before each new eruption of the volcano, the ground rises 3 feet (1 m) or more and then suddenly falls.

A narrow, deep trench is formed. This is a *very* slow collision, occurring over millions of years. Eventually, magma melts the edge of the oceanic plate. This process is called subduction. The amount of crust destroyed at convergent boundaries is about the same as the new crust being formed at divergent boundaries.

Subduction is not a smooth process. It is usually accompanied by violent earthquakes. This happens because pieces of the colliding plates may crack, become wedged in place for a while, and then move suddenly. Areas where ocean and continental plates converge may also produce active volcanoes.

As oceanic plates move apart, magma rises through the gap, cooling to form mountain chains along ocean ridges. The ocean plates move away from the ridge and toward the continental plates. When these plates collide, the ocean plate is driven downward into the mantle (subduction zone).

Subduction

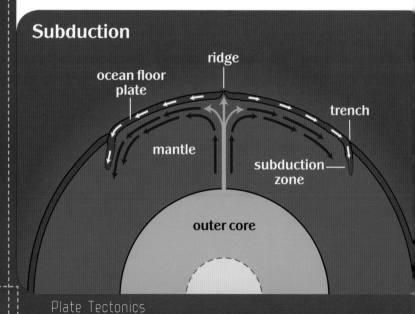

ocean floor plate

ridge

trench

mantle

subduction zone

outer core

This underwater photo was taken by a submarine at the Ring of Fire in the Pacific Ocean. It shows volcanic activity in the trench.

The huge trench that curves around the Pacific Ocean was formed in this way. It is nicknamed the Ring of Fire because earthquakes and volcanoes are very common there.

Collision of an oceanic plate with a continental plate can also form mountains. As the edge of the continental plate rides up over the subducted ocean plate, huge mountain ranges may be thrust up. The Andes Mountains of South America formed in this way. The South American Plate was lifted in a collision

The Andes Mountains in South America were formed when the South American Plate was lifted in a collision with the Nazca Plate.

with the smaller Nazca Plate in the Pacific Ocean, along the Peru-Chile trench.

Subduction allows the size of Earth's crust to stay the same, even while new crust is being formed by seafloor spreading. Some scientists believe that this, rather than convection in the mantle, is the main driving force in plate tectonics. In 1994 Japanese geologist Seiya Uyeda stated at an international conference that subduction plays the major role in "running the plate tectonic machinery." It is powered by the force of gravity. The colder, denser ocean plate sinks into the trench, dragging the rest of the plate with it.

When two ocean plates converge, usually one is subducted under the other, forming a trench. The Mariana Trench, the deepest in the world, was formed in a collision between the faster-moving Pacific Plate and the slower-moving Philippine Plate. Subduction between ocean plates produces underwater volcanoes. As these volcanoes build up, they may eventually form a curving chain of islands around the curve of the trench. Earthquakes also occur as the plates converge.

When two continental plates meet in a head-on collision, the results are spectacular. Both plates have about the same density, so neither one is likely to be subducted under the other. Instead, they crunch together, and their edges buckle upward or sideways, producing huge mountain ranges. The Himalayas, the highest mountain range in the world, were produced about 50 million years ago, when the Indian Plate crashed into the Eurasian Plate and eventually became attached to Asia. In the original supercontinent Pangaea, India had been joined to modern-day Africa. After the continents broke apart, the Indian Plate gradually drifted up to its present position. Fossils of sea creatures have been found atop the Himalayas—further evidence that these lands were once at the edge of an ocean.

This view of the Himalayas was taken by astronauts aboard the International Space Station as it orbits around Earth.

When two tectonic plates slide past each other, the area where they meet is called a transform boundary. Usually this kind of plate boundary connects two zones of spreading or two trenches formed by subduction. Most transform boundaries are in the oceans, but a few are found on land. The break in the rocks at a boundary between two tectonic plates is called a fault. At the San Andreas Fault in California, for example, the Pacific Plate is moving northwest and grinding against the North American Plate. This has been going on for 10 million years, at a rate of about 2 inches (5 cm) per year.

Small earthquakes may continually occur at transform boundaries, as Earth's crust adjusts for the shifts in position.

The San Andreas Fault is easily visible on Earth's surface in this photo taken near Carrizo Plain in Southern California.

Continents Adrift

The movements of the tectonic plates have produced dramatic changes in the conditions on the continents. Scientists believe that about 425 million years ago, most of Earth's landmasses were clustered in the southern half of the planet. North America and Europe were at the equator. By 250 million years ago, the landmasses had joined to form the supercontinent Pangaea. (For a map of continental drift, see page 19.)

About 200 million years ago, Pangaea began to break up. First, it split across the middle, into a northern continent, Laurasia, and a southern landmass, Gondwanaland. About 135 million years ago, Gondwanaland began to split. Africa and South America gradually moved apart, forming the Atlantic Ocean. Australia became an island touching Antarctica, and India split off from Africa and began to drift northward, toward Asia.

The splits continued. By about 65 million years ago, Laurasia was mostly separated into Eurasia and North America, but they were still joined in the far north by the landmass that is now the island of Greenland. When the split was completed, about 40 million years ago, Greenland had become an island. Meanwhile, Australia was beginning to move away from Antarctica.

The movements of the continents had some important effects on the animals, plants, and other creatures that lived on them. By about 225 million years ago, when Pangaea was still a single supercontinent, there were fish in the oceans, along with invertebrates, such as crabs and clams. A variety of plants and animals had begun to live on the lands. This was the start of the Age of Reptiles. Not only crocodiles, lizards, snakes, and other reptiles similar to current species but also giant dinosaurs were the dominant animals on land.

The first mammals were mouse-sized insect eaters. About 190 million years ago, they appeared in Gondwanaland. This southern continent had already separated from Laurasia, but there was still a land bridge between Africa and Eurasia at what is now the Strait of Gibraltar.

The earliest mammals laid eggs, like their reptile ancestors. Their two surviving descendants are the duckbilled platypus and the spiny anteater (echidna), which no longer live anywhere but Australia. The babies of later mammals developed—to a point— inside their mother's body. They were born while they were still very tiny and helpless and managed to crawl into a special pouch on their mother's belly. There,

The duckbilled platypus (below left) *and the spiny anteater* (below right) *are the only surviving descendants of mammals that laid eggs. They are both found only in Australia.*

Kangaroos are a kind of marsupial. Like the baby kangaroo shown here, their young finish their development in a pouch on their mother's body.

safe and protected, they finished their development while feeding on milk produced by their mother's mammary gland. Over many years, these primitive mammals, called marsupials, evolved into a great variety of species. Some, such as opossums and koalas, were able to climb trees. Others, such as kangaroos and wallabies, became specialized for jumping with long, strong hind legs and a long tail that helped them to balance while sailing through the air. There were also marsupial "mice," marsupial "cats," marsupial "wolves," and many others.

Marsupials were still the dominant mammals when Australia broke away from Gondwanaland. The island continent remained caught in a sort of "time warp." The marsupials stayed the same while mammals on the mainland evolved further, into placental mammals. Their young spent a much longer time developing inside the mother's body, nourished from her blood through an organ called the placenta. When they were born, they were much better equipped to survive. They competed successfully with marsupials for food and living space. Some marsupials in Africa and South America survived, and opossums migrated up to North America over a land bridge. But placental mammals soon greatly outnumbered the marsupials, except in Australia. No placental mammals lived on the Australian continent until the first human

Traveling Turtles

The continental drift theory has explained some puzzling animal behavior. After sea turtles hatch from their eggs, they toddle down the beach and swim out into the ocean. Years later, when they are ready to lay eggs of their own, the female turtles travel back to the same beach where they were born.

Green sea turtles that live and feed off the coast of Brazil in the twenty-first century do not lay their eggs on the beaches there. Instead, they swim 1,250 miles (2,000 km) to tiny Ascension Island in the middle of the Atlantic Ocean to make their nests. On this long voyage, they do not feed

This baby green sea turtle heads toward the ocean for the first time.

and they face many dangers. This seemed puzzling until scientists realized that tens of millions of years ago, the Atlantic Ocean was a lot smaller. Ascension Island was right off the coast of Brazil. At that time, it made sense for turtles feeding near the coast to swim across to a nearby island and lay their eggs where they would be safe from mainland predators. The trip got longer as the continents moved apart. But this happened very slowly (just a few centimeters each year), and the turtles had time to adapt. The lengthening trip helped the turtles to evolve. Those with strong flippers for swimming and large fat deposits to provide energy were more likely to survive the long journey and have offspring like themselves.

settlers brought dogs with them. The descendants of these dogs became wild and are today's Australian dingoes. Later human settlers introduced sheep, cattle, and rabbits.

Tectonic movements also explain some other peculiar observations. For example, there are monkeys

The Tale of the Horse

We know from fossil records that the first horses appeared about 60 million years ago, in North America. These first horses were dog-sized animals with five-toed feet. Scientists have named them *Eohippus*, which means "dawn horse." Gradually horses grew larger and became more specialized for running. Meanwhile, they spread to Europe, Asia, and Africa while connections between the continents still existed.

The present-day horse, *Equus*, developed by about three million years ago. During an ice age about eight thousand years ago, horses became extinct in North America, but they survived in the Old World. What about the mustangs, "native wild horses" in the United States? They were brought to America by Spanish adventurers in the sixteenth century.

in three continents: Asia, Africa, and South America. But the Old World monkeys of Asia and Africa are rather different from the New World monkeys that live in the South American jungles. The two lines developed in different ways after South America split off from Africa. Apes and our apelike ancestors developed from the Old World monkey line and never appeared in the Americas. Humans first migrated into North America from Asia about thirty thousand years ago over a land bridge that existed for a while after Siberia and Alaska bumped together.

Apes, like the baboon found in Africa (right), *developed from Old World monkeys. New World monkeys, like these capuchin monkeys* (below), *are found only in the jungles of South America.*

chapter five

Volcanoes: The Fire Within

Mount Saint Helens in Washington State was once famous for its nearly perfect dome shape. But that changed on May 18, 1980, when the top of the mountain exploded.

Mount Saint Helens is actually a volcano. It had been quiet for 123 years. But there were some warning signs that it was waking up. In mid-March of that year, small earthquakes shook the mountain. Soon steam blasted through the snow and ice at the peak. The explosion formed a large hole (a crater) that grew to 1,300 feet (396 m) wide in just a week. That was only the beginning.

The earthquakes continued, and cracks started to form on the mountain. By May 17, there had been more than ten thousand earthquakes! A big bulge, 450 feet (137 m) wide had formed on the side of the mountain. The next morning, right after a strong earthquake, the bulge burst. Rocks, ash, gases, and steam blasted up and out at 300 miles (483 km) per hour and then fell down to cover the surrounding area. The hot rocks and gases melted part of the ice cap. Water mixed with the rocks to form mud. Huge mudflows poured down the mountainside, knocking down trees and destroying bridges and homes in their path.

Mount Saint Helens (above) *in Washington was photographed the day before the May 18, 1980, eruption* (below left). Below right: *Mudflows poured down the mountainside.*

An aerial view shows the giant crater left after Mount Saint Helens erupted in May 1980.

An hour later, the volcano exploded again. This time superhot lava gushed out of the crater. During the hours that followed, Mount Saint Helens continued to erupt, pouring out bursts of steam, ash, gases, and hot rocks. By the end of the day, winds had blown more than 500 million tons (455 million metric tons) of ash eastward.

Mount Saint Helens had five more eruptions that summer and fall. More than a dozen more eruptions, lava flows, and mudslides occurred up to the fall of 1986. Then the mountain quieted down, only to wake up again in 2004. Small eruptions continued until January 2008. Scientists continue to watch Mount Saint Helens. They say it is one of the most dangerous volcanoes in the United States.

Where Did Volcanoes Get Their Name?

The word *volcano* comes from "Vulcan," the Roman god of fire. When an island near Sicily began to spit out puffs of smoke and fiery lava, the ancient Romans thought it was Vulcan's workshop. They believed that Vulcan was making weapons for the other gods. The thick gray cloud of ash was smoke from his furnace. The glowing rocks were sparks. The Romans called the island Vulcano. The word *volcano*, used to describe any mountain that can erupt, comes from this name. The mountain itself was formed by flows of lava during past eruptions.

What Is an Active Volcano?

Some volcanoes are very active. They continually rumble and puff out smoke, steam, and ash. Others have been quiet for as long as anyone can remember. However, volcanologists (scientists who study volcanoes) have found evidence in rocks that these volcanoes did erupt long ago. These scientists say a volcano is active if it is erupting or showing other signs of activity, such as earthquakes, puffs of smoke, or leaking of gases.

A volcano that has been quiet for a while—as long as a few thousand years—is said to be dormant. (This term comes from the French word for "sleeping.") A dormant volcano could become active sometime in the future.

Some volcanoes are believed to be extinct. They have not shown any signs of activity for many thousands of years. Volcanologists do not think these volcanoes will ever erupt again.

The Most Famous Volcanic Eruption

Pompeii, in southern Italy, was a pleasant and wealthy city in the first century A.D. The people who lived there—twenty thousand or so—were used to occasional earthquakes and didn't worry about any greater danger. They were not aware that Mount Vesuvius, across the bay, was a dormant volcano. On August 24, A.D. 79, however, Vesuvius suddenly erupted. Panic spread through the city and nearby towns. Rocks and ash rained down on Pompeii, piling up at a rate of 6 inches (15 cm) per hour. Then, suddenly, a choking cloud of hot gases, ash, and rock poured out of the mountain at tremendous speeds. No one in its path could escape.

When the eruption ended, nineteen hours after it began, the entire city of Pompeii was buried under a layer of ash 25 feet (8 m) deep. Heavy rains then turned the ash into solid concrete. Nearly seventeen hundred years later, archaeologists dug out the buried city. They found houses, furniture, statues, and jewelry. Hollows in the volcanic rock preserved the outlines of the volcano's two thousand victims—even the expressions on their faces.

Mount Vesuvius looms over ruins at modern-day Pompeii.

How Volcanoes Form

Ancient peoples thought volcanic eruptions were caused by fires. Even in the eighteenth century, many scientists thought they were caused by burning coal deposits underground. But they are actually the result of plate tectonic movements that start deep within Earth's mantle.

A volcano starts out in the upper part of the mantle, where the rocks have melted into magma. Hot magma may ooze upward through gaps or cracks in the solid crust. Magma tends to rise because it contains some gases and is lighter than the rocks. As it melts the surrounding rock, the magma may form a magma chamber. This is a giant pool of magma under the surface. The magma in the chamber is under high pressure from the heavy weight of the crust above it. (Pressure is a pushing force.) Finally, the magma breaks through the surface and bursts out in an eruption.

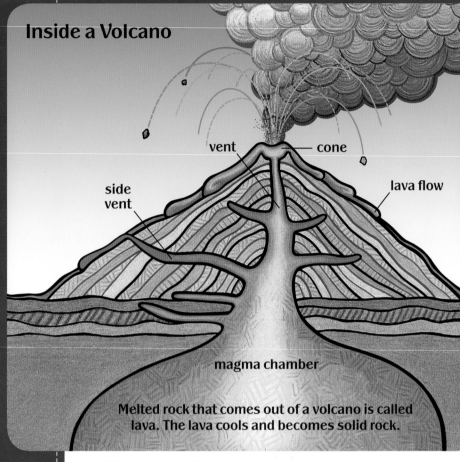

Inside a Volcano

vent — cone

side vent

lava flow

magma chamber

Melted rock that comes out of a volcano is called lava. The lava cools and becomes solid rock.

When a volcano "blows its top," melted rock erupts out of the magma chamber through an opening and flows out as lava. Hot gases, ash, and rocks also shoot up into the air.

The openings from which gases, lava, and other volcanic matter escape are called vents. In many volcanoes, the vent ends in a bowl-shaped crater at the top of the mountain. Some volcanoes also have vents on the side of the mountain.

About fifty to sixty volcanoes on land erupt each year and many more under the oceans. In

Under Pressure

Have you ever shaken a can of soda before opening it? Like the magma under Earth's surface, a can of soda contains a mixture of liquid and gas under pressure. When you pull the tab to open the can, the pressure on the gas (carbon dioxide) drops suddenly. The gas expands rapidly, and bubbly soda explodes out, all over everything. That is a lot like what happens when a volcano erupts. While it is still trapped under rock, the hot magma is also under great pressure. When it reaches the surface, that pressure is suddenly removed. That is why a huge cloud of hot gas, ash, and rocks may shoot up into the air when a volcano erupts.

fact, there are even active volcanoes erupting violently on the Arctic Ocean bottom, deep under the ice cover. Most of the world's volcanoes are found along boundaries where tectonic plates are bumping together or moving apart. However, some, such as the Hawaiian Islands, are in the middle of tectonic plates. They are parts of a chain of volcanic mountains strung out in the middle of the Pacific Ocean, nearly 2,000 miles (3,200 km) from the nearest plate boundary. Some of the volcanoes are extinct, but others have been active for quite a long time.

Why are some volcanoes so far from plate boundaries? In 1963 J. Tuzo Wilson, a Canadian geologist, suggested that

An Island Is Born

On November 14, 1963, off the southwest coast of Iceland, fishers watched an amazing sight: a volcanic eruption blasting out of the water. The eruption began about 425 feet (130 m) beneath the ocean surface. It continued for the next three and a half years. During that time, the lava flowing out of the volcano gradually built up an island with an area of 1 square mile (2.5 sq. km), whose peak rose more than 550 feet (169 m) above sea level. This new island was named Surtsey, after Surtur, a fire giant from Icelandic legend.

deep in the mantle are certain small, exceptionally hot regions. These hotspots, as they are called, rise through the mantle and heat the portion of the plate just above them, melting rock and forming a volcano. Thus, the Hawaiian Islands formed as the Pacific Plate slowly moved over a hotspot deep in the mantle. Over long ages of time, this hotspot produced one volcano after another. Each one erupted for a while, gradually building up a mountain high enough to rise above sea level and produce an island, and then became extinct as the plate moved past the hotspot and a new volcano formed farther down the chain.

Only scientists are allowed to visit the island of Surtsey. Since its birth, researchers have watched the island grow and develop. In 1965 plants became the first signs of life on Surtsey. They sprouted from seeds carried to the island by ocean currents or dropped by birds from nearby islands. Now much of the island is covered by plants—at least sixty different kinds have been found. In 1970 a bird was found nesting and raising its young in the warm lava. Since then a variety of insects and birds have made Surtsey their home. Sea animals that live nearby include seals, sea stars, and sea urchins.

The volcanic island of Surtsey lies off the coast of Iceland. It started forming in 1963, when a volcano underwater erupted for more than three years.

When a Volcano Erupts

Not all eruptions are huge explosions. In fact, they are often rather quiet events. And a volcano may have a different kind of eruption each time. How a volcano erupts actually depends on the pressure that builds inside the magma. Thick, gooey magma is under more pressure than thin, loose magma. The greater the pressure, the more explosive the eruption.

Lava spreads out onto the landscape in Hawaii.

When the magma is thin and runny, gas can escape easily. So instead of exploding during an eruption, lava flows gently down the sides of the volcano. Like a glowing, red-hot river, it may spread out over great distances. This is the least dangerous type of eruption. People usually have time to run for safety. The Hawaiian Islands generally have these mild eruptions.

When magma is really thick and sticky, like tar, it traps gas bubbles inside. The gas keeps building up until finally it explodes. The powerful eruption throws hot molten (melted) rock everywhere, and thick lava oozes out.

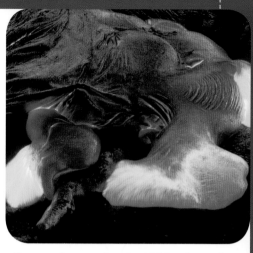

Some volcanoes develop thicker lava that oozes out after an eruption.

The most dangerous, explosive type of eruption happens when the magma is so thick and sticky that it acts like glue. As the magma at the top cools down, it becomes solid rock, plugging up the crater like a cork in a bottle. Over time—perhaps hundreds of years—the pressure underneath this plug keeps building. Eventually it bursts in a huge explosion! That's what happened when Mount Saint Helens erupted in May 1980.

Sometimes a plugged volcano calms down and becomes extinct. In some very old extinct volcanoes, the outer part of the mountain has been worn away so that only the plug remains.

What Comes Out of an Erupting Volcano?

An explosive eruption blasts gases, lava, and hot pieces of rock into the air with tremendous force. The gases that spew out of a volcano are mostly water and carbon dioxide. But there are also small amounts of poisonous gases. These include sulfur compounds, which are very stinky.

What Is Lava?

Lava is actually magma that has reached Earth's surface. It comes out as hot molten rock and burns up everything it touches—trees, houses, buildings, and people. The lava begins to cool as it flows down the sides of the volcano. Eventually it hardens and becomes solid rock.

Lavas may contain chemicals that give them various colors. Basalt, for example, is rock formed by dark-colored lava, either black or gray. Rhyolite is light colored, from white to pale gray, greenish, pink, or tan. The lava in Yellowstone National Park is rhyolite.

Below left: *These basalt hills in Washington State look like huge stairsteps because several lava flows piled on top of one another.* **Below right:** *This tan-colored rhyolite is near the Yellowstone River in Yellowstone National Park.*

Krakatoa, an active volcano in Indonesia, spews gases into the air.

(Some of them smell like rotten eggs.) The gases released by very explosive volcanic eruptions may shoot up high into the stratosphere, to as much as 30 miles (50 km) above Earth's surface. They may remain there for several years.

The broken-up rocks and other bits of volcanic matter are called pyroclastic material. (*Pyroclastic* comes from Greek words meaning "broken by fire.") This material can come in all sorts of shapes and sizes:

- Lapilli are tiny pieces of rock.
- Lava bombs are soft lumps. Most are somewhat rounded, about the size of a tennis ball.
- Volcanic blocks are solid chunks of rock. They can be really huge—as big as a car or a house. They can fall miles from the volcano and cause a lot of damage.

Did You Know?

Since 1990 more than eighty commercial airplanes have flown through volcanic ash clouds. Several of them almost crashed because the ash clogged their engines. But the pilots managed to get their engines started again and land safely.

Pyroclastic material also includes volcanic ash. It is hard and scratchy, not like the soft ash from a wood fire. The volcanic ash forms a huge cloud that may stretch for miles above the crater. As the ash falls to the ground, it can cover a whole area like a blanket of snow. It is dangerous to people because it can make it difficult to breathe.

Eruptions can also cause gases, hot ash, and pieces of rock to race down the sides of the volcano. These pyroclastic flows can travel as fast as 100 to 150 miles (161 to 241 km) per hour.

As the lava, ash, and rocks spill over the sides of the mountain, they harden into solid rock. Each eruption adds material to the mountain, and it gradually gets taller. Very violent eruptions, however, can blast away the rock and tear part of the mountain down. For example, the big eruption of Mount Saint Helens in 1980 blasted a huge crater out of the top of the mountain. Afterward, a series of mild eruptions helped to build a dome inside the crater. The dome was torn down twice by powerful eruptions and then built up again. But the mountain peak is still much lower than it was before the 1980 eruption.

The Year without a Summer

Mount Tambora, in Indonesia, erupted in 1815 with the power of millions of nuclear bombs. Before the cone-shaped mountain "blew its top," it was 14,000 feet (4,300 m) high. After the eruption, it was nearly 4,600 feet (1,400 m) lower, topped by a hollowed-out crater more than 4 miles (7 km) wide. The explosion itself and the huge tsunamis—sea waves—that it produced killed about ten thousand people. Another eighty-two thousand died as a result of starvation and disease in the following years because thick ash deposits had buried all the farmlands in the area.

Actually, Mount Tambora's eruption affected the whole world. Clouds of dust and gases covered Earth for years, partly blocking out the sunlight. In 1816 it snowed during the summer months in many parts of the United States and Europe. That frigid time was known as "the year without a summer."

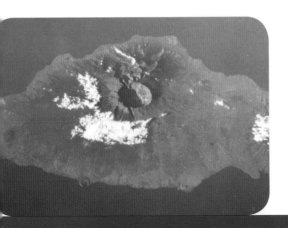

The giant hole left by the eruption of Mount Tambora as seen from a space shuttle. The volcano's eruption in 1815 affected weather around the world.

Kinds of Volcanoes

Not all volcanoes are cone-shaped. Depending on the way they erupt, volcanoes can form different kinds of structures. The main ones include:

Cinder cone volcano: This is the most common type of volcano. It is formed by loose pieces of lava that fall as cinders close to a single vent. The lava cinders pile up around the vent, producing a steep-sided cone shape. Usually a crater is at the top. An example is Parícutin, in Mexico. This volcano first appeared in 1943 and built up a 1,200-foot (366 m) cone in just nine years.

Shield volcano: This kind of volcano is wide, with gently sloping sides. It looks like an ancient warrior's shield. It is formed by a series of slow-

The Parícutin volcano in Mexico appeared as a hole in a farmer's field in 1943 and continued erupting for eight more years. The volcano's ash and lava buried two villages nearby.

Plate Tectonics

The Hawaiian Islands, shown above in a satellite image, are all shield volcanoes. The largest volcano in Hawaii, Mauna Loa, is shown below in a photo from a space shuttle. Dark lava flows can be seen on the sides of the volcano.

moving lava flows. The Hawaiian Islands are made of a long chain of shield volcanoes. One of them is Mauna Loa, the world's largest active volcano.

Composite volcano: This type is also called a stratovolcano. It is a large, steep-sided volcano that is formed by a series of eruptions. Layers of lava flow over buildups of cinders and ash and then are covered by more cinders and ash. Lava may also ooze out through cracks in the sides of the mountain. Composite volcanoes are often the most deadly. Examples are Mount Saint Helens in Washington State, Krakatoa in Indonesia, and Mount Pinatubo in the Philippines.

Mount Pinatubo in the Philippines is a composite volcano. The last major eruption in 1991 affected weather across the planet.

Mont Pelée in the Caribbean is dormant in modern times but last erupted in 1902. The eruption killed thirty thousand people, destroying the largest city in the island nation of Martinique.

Lava dome volcano: This kind of volcano is formed when very slow-flowing lava piles up around the vent. The dome grows as the pool of magma inside expands. The outer surface cools and breaks apart, spilling out volcanic matter down the sides. Lava domes often form in the craters or on the sides of large composite volcanoes. Examples are Mont Pelée in Martinique, in the Caribbean, and the lava dome that has formed inside the crater of Mount Saint Helens.

Crater Lake in Oregon is a giant caldera—the collapsed magma chamber of a volcano.

Caldera volcano: This kind of volcano may be formed when a huge eruption empties the magma chamber. The ground above the chamber collapses into the emptied space, forming a large, bowl-like hollow called a caldera. The caldera may later fill with water, forming a lake. Crater Lake in Oregon is an example of a caldera volcano. It is 6 miles (10 km) across and almost 2,000 feet (600 m) deep. Some calderas remain very active, with frequent earthquakes, cracks in the ground, and raising or lowering of the ground level. Hot springs and geysers may also appear. They may remain active for months, years, or even centuries.

Are Geysers Volcanoes?

No. What erupts from a geyser is boiling-hot water and steam, not lava and ash. However, geysers are usually found near active volcanoes. The water in underground springs close to a volcano's magma chamber heats up. Pressure rises inside it until a spray of hot water squirts out through a crack in the ground. That lowers the pressure in the hot spring, and the geyser stops erupting until the water pressure builds up again. The most famous geyser is Old Faithful, in Yellowstone National Park. It erupts fairly regularly, every ninety-one minutes on average, sending 3,700 to 8,400 gallons (14,000 to 32,000 liters) of water more than 100 feet (30 m) into the air.

Old Faithful blows its top in Yellowstone National Park in Wyoming. Millions of visitors tour the park every year and wait for Old Faithful to erupt.

Some erupting volcanoes do not form mountains. In flood eruptions, runny lava may spread out for hundreds or even thousands of miles. The lava flows may erupt from many different cracks in Earth's crust over a large area. Instead of forming a mountain, this kind of eruption builds up a large plain or plateau. The Columbia River Plateau, which covers much of Oregon, Washington, and Idaho, was built up in this way. It extends over an area of 100,000 square miles (260,000 sq. km).

The Columbia River and a part of the Columbia River Plateau are visible in this photo of the Oregon town of The Dalles. The plateau extends into Idaho and Washington.

Dante II into the Inferno

Samples of the hot gases released in volcanic eruptions can provide valuable information, but collecting them is a very dangerous job. In 1993, for example, eight volcanologists were killed during on-the-spot studies of erupting volcanoes. Researchers at Carnegie Mellon Institute, working with NASA (National Aeronautics and Space Administration), designed and built an eight-legged walking robot to take over this dangerous job. It seemed natural to name the robot Dante, after a thirteenth-century Italian poet, Dante Alighieri. His most famous poem was *The Inferno*, an account of an imagined trip down into Hell.

The first Dante robot started down into Mount Erebus, a live volcano in Antarctica, in 1992. But the long cable connecting Dante to its remote controls broke, and the robot fell into the volcano. In 1994 an improved version, Dante II, was able to explore the Mount Spurr volcano in Alaska. Dante II even went down the steep crater walls to gather gas samples from the crater floor. Space researchers from NASA hope someday to use robots like Dante II to explore the harsh terrains of other planets.

chapter six

Earthquakes: On Shaky Ground

On October 17, 1989, the third game of the World Series was about to start at Candlestick Park in San Francisco, California. It was a battle between two California baseball teams, the Oakland Athletics and the San Francisco Giants. During warm-ups, just minutes before game time, the television signal started to break up. Then suddenly viewers heard sportscaster Al Michaels yell out, "I'll tell you what—we're having an earth—," and the TV screen went blank. Minutes later, the TV network switched to a telephone connection. Al Michaels spoke to the TV audience, explaining that there was a power outage due to an earthquake that hit the San Francisco Bay area.

When the earthquake hit, the stadium rumbled with such tremendous force, it felt like a bomb had exploded. The shaking lasted for only fifteen

Above: *Crowds mill around in Candlestick Park after an earthquake shook the stadium in October 1989.* Below: *One fan cowered behind his seat after the earthquake. Soon everyone had to leave the stadium.*

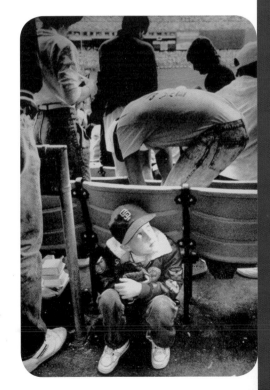

seconds, but it seemed much longer. No one was hurt inside Candlestick Park, but everyone had to leave. Meanwhile, the earthquake and the smaller quakes that followed it caused damage over a wide area of northern California.

The World Series earthquake is officially known as the Loma Prieta earthquake. Loma Prieta is a mountain in northern California, located in the Santa Cruz Mountains.

The World Series earthquake, as it is often called, was the first strong earthquake in the United States to be shown on live television.

The earthquake started in the Loma Prieta region and caused serious damage as far as 60 miles (95 km) away. Near the Santa Cruz Mountains, many houses were completely destroyed. In San Francisco and Oakland, huge cracks split through sidewalks, roadways, and parking lots. Buildings crumbled. Broken gas lines started huge fires.

More than forty people died when the Cypress Bridge on Interstate 880 in Oakland collapsed. A huge section of the San Francisco-Oakland Bay Bridge broke off as well. The earthquake set off many landslides and rockfalls down the mountainsides.

A collapsed section of the San Francisco–Oakland Bay Bridge is shown a few days after the earthquake.

Destruction from the Great San Francisco earthquake of 1906 included this cobblestone street. It cracked down the middle during the quake, and a wooden cart fell into the gap.

Was Loma Prieta the "Big One?"

Scientists say no. The deadliest earthquake in U.S. history was the Great San Francisco earthquake of 1906. It had an estimated magnitude of 7.8. (A quake higher than magnitude 7 is a major earthquake.) Much of the city was destroyed, not because of the earthquake itself but because of the huge fires that broke out. Broken water lines made it hard to fight the fires, so they raged on for four days. At least 3,000 people died in this disaster, and about 225,000 were left homeless.

Since the Great San Francisco earthquake of 1906, scientists have been saying that the next "big one" would hit California within the next hundred years or so. The Loma Prieta earthquake of 1989 was not powerful enough to be the "big one." It had a magnitude of only 6.9—not big enough to qualify as a "major earthquake."

Did You Know?

Every year, Southern
California has
about ten thousand
earthquakes. But
most of them are
too weak for people
to feel them.

One major highway was blocked so badly that it had to be closed to traffic for a month. All together, the Loma Prieta earthquake killed 63 people and injured 3,757.

Every year, scientists detect roughly five hundred thousand earthquakes worldwide. Many of them go unnoticed because they are weak. An estimated one hundred thousand quakes can be felt, but only about one hundred are strong enough to cause damage.

What Causes Earthquakes?

Most earthquakes occur at plate boundaries, at the edges of tectonic plates. Nearly half of all earthquakes occur in subduction zones. In these areas, two plates move toward each other and collide. The edge of one plate slips under the edge of the other. Earthquakes also occur at transform boundaries. Here two plates are moving sideways past each other. Earthquakes can occur at divergent boundaries as well, where plates are moving apart and seafloor spreading is occurring. These earthquakes are often associated with volcanic activity.

When tectonic plates move, their movement puts stress on the rocks near plate boundaries. Stress builds up and causes faults (cracks) in Earth's crust. Most earthquakes occur in the fault regions at plate boundaries. Eventually, the rock breaks under the stress, and the ground at the surface shakes. Scientists call these ground-shaking tremors.

Most faults develop underground—from 50 miles (80 km) to as much as 500 miles (805 km) deep! But some can actually be seen on the surface. One famous example is the San Andreas Fault, a transform boundary that runs down two-thirds of the length of California. (This fault was involved in the 1989 World Series earthquake and in the Great San Francisco earthquake of 1906 as well.)

Some parts of the San Andreas Fault move slowly and steadily. These slow, creeping movements produce frequent small or moderate earthquakes. In other parts of the fault,

The San Andreas Fault in California is one fault that can actually be seen on the surface of Earth. This fault is involved in many of the earthquakes in California.

pieces of the plates get locked together and can't slide as the plates move. Stresses build up on both sides of the fault for tens or hundreds of years and then produce devastating earthquakes. (The buildup and sudden release of stress is very much like what happens when you stretch a rubber band until it breaks.) The same thing happens at other faults around the world.

Why Do Tectonic Plates Get Locked Together?

When tectonic plates rub against one another, they produce friction. This is a force that works against movement. For example, friction stops a moving car when the driver presses on the brake. Friction between tectonic plates can lock them together.

Earthquake Belts

Earthquakes are most common in three main "earthquake belts" in different parts of the world. About 81 percent of the world's largest earthquakes occur along the Ring of Fire. This earthquake belt is shaped like a horseshoe and curves around the Pacific Ocean, from the west coast of South America, up through Alaska, and all the way down to New Zealand.

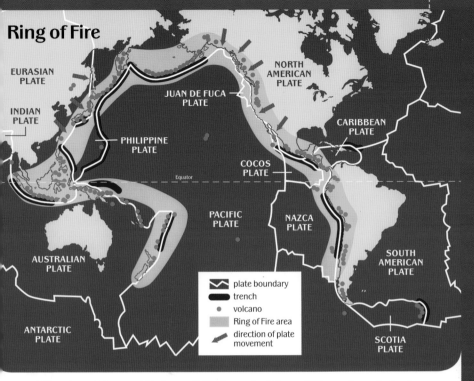

There's nothing pacific (peaceful) about the Ring of Fire, a huge belt of volcano and earthquake activity that nearly surrounds the Pacific Ocean. The belt traces the outlines of boundaries between moving tectonic plates.

The second main earthquake zone, known as the Alpide belt, has 17 percent of the world's largest earthquakes. This belt stretches from Indonesia through the Himalayas, across Iran and Turkey, and west through the Mediterranean region.

The third main earthquake belt lies along the Mid-Atlantic Ridge. Other earthquakes are scattered in various parts of the world. In these areas, earthquakes occur along faults that are far away from plate boundaries. In the United States, a famous example is the New Madrid Fault in Missouri. This fault is in the middle of the North American Plate.

Ancient Earthquake Explanations

Many ancient peoples believed that earthquakes were a punishment for something they had done to displease the gods. The ancient Greeks, for example, believed that Poseidon, the god of the sea, caused earthquakes when he was angry with the mortals on Earth. According to another Greek myth, the giant Atlas held the planet on his shoulders. When he got tired and moved his shoulders, an earthquake occurred. The Japanese, living on volcanic islands in an earthquake zone, thought a catfish held the world on its back. A god was

Volcanic earthquakes can also occur within tectonic plates, far from their edges. Such earthquakes, which are usually rather small, generally occur just before and during volcanic activity. These quakes are caused by the pressure placed on rocks in the crust as magma forces its way toward the surface. For example, in the weeks before Mount Saint Helens in Washington State erupted in May 1980, there were thousands of small earthquakes.

Other earthquakes within tectonic plates occur in areas where the ground is soft and may be under great stress from temperature and pressure changes in the rocks beneath. Three powerful earthquakes that assigned to watch it, but sometimes his attention wandered and the fish wriggled, shaking the planet. Other ancient peoples believed that Earth was held up by giant pigs, turtles, oxen, or snakes. They believed that an earthquake occurred when the animals moved.

In the fourth century B.C., the Greek philosopher and scientist Aristotle looked for a more scientific explanation. He thought that violent winds, trapped beneath Earth's surface, sometimes burst out, producing an earthquake. Scientists believed this theory for more than two thousand years.

struck New Madrid, Missouri, in 1811 and 1812 were quakes of this kind. They caused the Mississippi River to change its course and were felt 1,000 miles (1,600 km) away.

Human activities can cause earthquakes too. When a new dam is built, huge amounts of water build up behind towering walls. This puts a great deal of pressure on a relatively small area. If a fault is nearby and rocks are already under stress, the added pressure may cause them to slip. Earthquakes have occurred in the areas of the Hoover Dam in the United States, the Aswan High Dam in Egypt, and a number of others. Large nuclear explosions, set off underground, have led to earthquakes. So has the pumping of wastes or other fluids deep into the ground. Earthquakes occurred, for example, when waste fluids from the city of Denver, Colorado, were pumped into deep wells east of the city. After the pumping was stopped, the earthquakes soon also stopped.

What Happens During an Earthquake?

As stresses build up at a boundary between two colliding tectonic plates, the rocks begin to bend and bulge. Like a stretched rubber band, rocks can absorb a certain amount of stress. But eventually they break or slip into a new position, setting off vibrations in Earth's crust.

The place where the rocks break or move is called the focus of the earthquake. It is usually deep underground—from dozens to hundreds of miles (km) below the surface. The spot on the surface directly above the focus is called the epicenter of the earthquake. It is there that the most severe damage usually occurs. The vibrations, called seismic waves, spread out from the focus in all directions.

Seismic waves come in two main forms: body waves and surface waves. Body waves move through Earth's inner layers. Surface waves travel only through Earth's outermost layers—the crust and the upper part of the mantle.

Body waves are the first seismic waves to arrive during an earthquake. There are two types of body waves: primary waves (P waves) and secondary waves (S waves).

Earthquake Waves

surface waves:
slow and rocking

epicenter

focus

P (body) waves:
compress and stretch

S (body) waves: up and
down or side to side

seismic waves

P waves and S waves are two different ways that energy from earth-quakes can move through a solid. These body waves move through Earth's inner layers and are the fastest-moving. Surface waves travel over the surface of the crust and are slower.

P waves are the fastest. Speeding along at 15,000 miles (24,140 km) per hour, P waves move through solid rock, air, and liquids, such as water and magma. The waves push and pull the rock, like the movement in a Slinky toy.

S waves are the second type of seismic wave to arrive. S waves are slower. They can move only through solid materials, at a speed of about 9,000 miles (14,484 km) per hour. They make side-to-side or up-and-down movements, like ocean waves.

As the body waves travel underground, away from the focus, the P waves cause the rocks to be pushed and pulled. Buildings rocked by these waves shake up and down because the waves are arriving from below. Then come the S waves, which cause rocks and buildings to move from side to side.

Early Warning

Sometimes animals can sense when an earthquake is coming. Dogs may bark wildly for no obvious reason. Ducks and geese leave their ponds. Caged birds fly against the sides of their cages. Fish come to the surface in great numbers. These animals can hear the P waves coming. Humans can't hear earthquake waves. They just feel the shaking.

Surface waves are the last to arrive. People feel them as slow, rocking movements. Usually these waves cause the most damage during an earthquake. If the earthquake is deep underground, however, surface waves will have little effect. There are two types of surface waves: Love waves and Rayleigh waves.

Love waves are faster. They move the ground from side to side as they travel through Earth's surface.

Rayleigh waves move more slowly. They roll along Earth's surface like waves on the ocean. As they

How Long Do Earthquakes Last?

Most earthquakes last for less than fifteen seconds, but rare ones may go on for a minute or more. The longest-lasting earthquake ever recorded was about ten minutes. It occurred on December 26, 2004, off the coast of Indonesia and caused a huge, destructive tsunami (powerful ocean wave caused by earthquakes under or near the ocean).

roll along, the Rayleigh waves move the ground up and down and side to side in the same direction the wave is moving.

Before the main earthquake, sometimes there are one or more rather small earthquakes, called foreshocks. After the main earthquake, there are often additional, small quakes, called aftershocks. They follow immediately after the main earthquake and may continue for days, weeks, months, or even years. Generally, aftershocks are weaker than the main earthquake. But sometimes, if the aftershock is close to a heavily populated area, it may cause more damage than the main quake. Aftershocks usually occur because only part of the stress built up in the rocks was released by the main earthquake.

Most of the destruction during a major earthquake is caused by the shaking and trembling ground. The severe stresses created by these motions can collapse many structures that have not been reinforced enough to make them earthquake-proof. Avalanches and landslides can also cause damage, burying entire towns. In cities broken gas lines or flammable items shaken down onto hot stoves can start fires that sweep through whole neighborhoods. Broken water lines may hamper the efforts of the firefighters.

Above: *This photo shows the destruction after the Tangshan earthquake in China in 1976.* Left: *The earthquake in Kobe, Japan, in 1995 left roads twisted and buildings in ruins.*

The Worst Earthquake Ever?

Suddenly the ground shook. Hundreds of thousands of people were wakened from their sleep. Their buildings were trembling. Roads ripped open, swallowing cars like tiny toys. Gas lines snapped, starting thousands of fires throughout the city. Buildings swayed, then came crashing to the ground. People raced into the streets, shivering with fear.

The place was Kobe, Japan. The date: January 17, 1995. An earthquake had devastated the city. Although the tremors lasted only twelve seconds, more than 5,500 people died. In addition, more than 190,000 buildings were destroyed or badly damaged, leaving more than 300,000 people homeless. The city had been one of the most active seaports in the world, but the earthquake destroyed most of its docks. The Japanese government had to spend close to $150 billion to repair the damage in Kobe.

Devastating as it was, however, the Kobe earthquake was far from the worst in history. In fact, the Great Kanto earthquake, which hit Japan in 1923, killed 143,000 people in Tokyo and the nearby area. The 1976 Tangshan earthquake in the Hebei Province of China killed more than 250,000 people.

Since most big earthquakes are associated with faults located under or near the ocean, another destructive force is often unleashed. Powerful ocean waves called tsunamis can form. Earthquakes that occur on the ocean floor can send out powerful waves through the water and up to the surface, causing the nearby ocean waters to swell. While still at sea, tsunamis may be only 2 to 3 feet (0.6 to 0.9 m) high. A ship might pass over one and not notice it at all. But as these waves approach the shore, they can build up to enormous heights—up to 100 feet (30 m)!

Tsunamis can travel as fast as a jet plane, at

The devastating "Christmas tsunami" is shown hitting the coast of Thailand on December 26, 2004. The tsunami was sparked by an underwater earthquake off the coast of nearby Indonesia.

speeds exceeding 500 miles (800 km) per hour. They are often so powerful that they can move many miles inland and flood villages and towns on the way.

A huge underwater earthquake near Indonesia in December 2004 triggered tsunamis all along the coasts of the Indian Ocean. The waves reached heights of up to 100 feet (30 m) and resulted in more than 250,000 deaths in eleven countries. India, Indonesia, Sri Lanka, and Thailand were the hardest hit.

Made in Japan

Tsunami is a Japanese word meaning "harbor wave." Japan has had more than its share—at least fifteen devastating tsunamis in the past three hundred years. Japan is located in an especially active earthquake region because it lies where four tectonic plates meet.

Measuring Earthquakes

Earthquakes occur every day somewhere within our planet. Many thousands of earthquakes are detected each year. However, most quakes are so faint that even the best instruments do not detect them.

Seismologists detect, measure, and study earthquakes, using seismographs. These instruments work by measuring the movement of the ground and how fast the seismic waves are moving. Some seismographs can detect the seismic waves that form when rocks move beneath Earth's surface, even ones that have formed thousands of miles away.

The First Seismograph

A Chinese scientist, Chang Heng, invented an instrument for detecting earthquakes back in A.D. 132. A pendulum in the center was attached to a ring of eight dragon heads, each of which held a bronze ball in its mouth. Eight statues of toads with open mouths sat directly below the dragons. If an earthquake occurred, the first tremors set the pendulum swinging. Then a ball dropped from one of the dragons into the mouth of the toad beneath it. The toad that caught the ball indicated the direction of the earthquake.

The first seismograph (pictured here) was invented by Chinese scientist Chang Heng in A.D. 132.

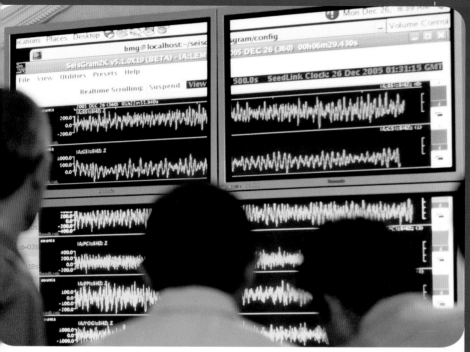

These scientists are studying seismograms on computer screens. Many newer seismographs record measurements on computers instead of paper.

Others contain devices called tiltmeters. These instruments can detect tiny ground movements that may signal an oncoming earthquake. When seismic waves are detected, a seismograph produces wavy lines that are recorded on computers.

Two different scales are used to measure earthquakes: the Richter scale and the Mercalli scale. The Richter magnitude scale gives a number rating showing the earthquake's power or "magnitude." The higher the number, the bigger the earthquake. An earthquake with a magnitude up to 2 can be detected only by instruments. At a Richter magnitude of 3 to 4, hanging lights sway and there may be minor damage. At magnitude 5 to 6, dishes, books, or other objects may fall off shelves and walls of buildings may crack. An earthquake with a magnitude of 7 or greater is considered "major." It can make buildings collapse and cause highways and bridges to buckle and twist. The earthquake that struck Sichuan Province in China in May 2008, for example, measured 8 on the Richter scale. It caused huge destruction because its seismic waves traveled great distances through the firm lands of central China, without losing their power.

An earthquake in May 2008 devastated buildings and roads in Sichuan Province in China. Nearly seventy thousand people died in the quake.

Superquakes

The devastating earthquake in the Indian Ocean in December 2004 had a magnitude of 9.1 to 9.3—the second largest in recorded history. The largest, with a magnitude of 9.5, occurred in Chile on May 22, 1960. No earthquakes with a magnitude greater than 10 have ever been detected.

The Modified Mercalli Intensity scale is based on an earthquake's effects, rather than its power. It applies only to populated areas. Seismologists use observations rather than instruments to make an intensity rating.

The Mercalli scale has a 12-point rating scale. The higher the number, the higher the intensity. For example, a rating of 2 points indicates a barely noticeable earthquake. An earthquake with a Mercalli intensity of 10 points causes major damage to buildings, bridges, and other structures. An earthquake has different effects in different areas. So there are always different intensity values measured from one earthquake.

Mercalli scores are not as scientific as Richter magnitudes. They are based on people's descriptions and ratings of damage, rather than by recorded waves on a seismograph. Moreover, the amount of damage depends on the distance from the epicenter, the structures of the buildings, and the kind of material they rest on. A building resting on solid rock, for example, usually will not shake as much as one built on sand.

chapter seven

Plate Tectonics and the Future

Some geologists predict that someday the California coast will snap off at the San Andreas Fault and drift into the Pacific Ocean. For a while, that portion of California will be an island, they say. Eventually, it will disappear into the deep trench off Alaska in the Aleutian Islands chain.

Other experts argue, however, that this won't happen because the San Andreas Fault is only about 9 miles (15 km) deep. That is just a quarter of the thickness of Earth's crust in that area—not enough to cause such a split. Moreover, the continental crust on which California sits is not very dense. It floats high above the mantle, like an iceberg rising high above the surface of the ocean.

Geologists do agree, however, that the Atlantic Ocean widens each year, while the Pacific Ocean continues to narrow. Eventually, the North American continent may merge with Asia as Alaska slowly crunches into Siberia. Meanwhile, Africa will drift northward, squeezing the Mediterranean Sea into a narrow channel. Because of cracks that are widening, East Africa may split off from the mainland, creating a new sea. Of course, all these things will take a

Heading for California

Satellite measurements suggest that Australia is currently moving toward California. Of course, it is not expected to get there very soon, since it is moving at a rate of about 2 inches (5 cm) per year. The continent is moving because a crack in the Indian Ocean floor is gradually widening. Within a few million years, however, Australia's progress will be slowed and its direction shifted by the huge Pacific Plate that lies southwest of California.

hundred million years or more to happen. What effects will plate tectonics have for the near future, within the lifetimes of modern people?

Can Earthquakes and Volcanic Eruptions Be Predicted?

In 1975 Chinese seismologists correctly predicted that an earthquake was about to strike the Chinese city of Haicheng. They based their prediction on observations of unusual animal behavior, changes in land and groundwater levels, and a series of increasingly strong and frequent foreshocks. Officials ordered the evacuation of the cities and villages in the area, and 90,000 people left their homes. Two days later, an earthquake measuring 7.3 on the Richter scale destroyed nine out of ten buildings in the area, but not a single person died. The following year, however, an earthquake struck Tangshan, a major industrial center in northern China with a population of more than 1 million. It caught everyone by surprise. More than 250,000 people died in that quake. By the late twentieth century, earthquake prediction was still rather unreliable.

Japan has been especially concerned about earthquake prediction. About one hundred thousand earthquakes occur there each year. Back in 1965, Japan set up a major plan to develop earthquake prediction methods. The program has concentrated especially on the Tokai region southwest of Tokyo, where three tectonic plates meet and there has not been a major earthquake since 1854. Figuring Tokai was overdue for a magnitude 8 earthquake—a "big one"—seismologists set up underground detectors to measure stress in the rocks all over the area. Four seismic stations equipped with tiltmeters were also set up on the nearby seafloor. The system has been expanded to link about one thousand seismographs throughout Japan with a fast computer network. It measures the fast-moving primary waves and calculates their location and strength within a few seconds. The aim is to send out warnings before the slower-moving secondary waves that cause most of the damage arrive.

Starting in 2007, an automated system began working. It flashes warnings on Japan's major TV channels, as well as radio stations and mobile phones. How early a warning people have depends on how far they are from the earthquake. If a big quake hits the

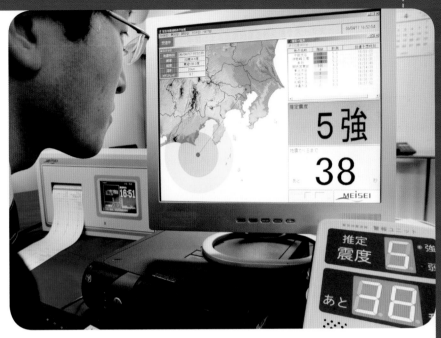

An engineer looks at a computer screen during a demonstration of Japan's automated system to give people early warnings for earthquakes.

Tokai region, for example, residents of Shizuoka, the closest city, will have about ten seconds warning. People in Tokyo, about 62 miles (100 km) away, will have about forty seconds warning before the shaking starts. That doesn't sound like much, but it may be enough for people to get to a safer place. In addition, commercial companies are producing systems that link into the network and automatically stop heavy factory machinery, stop trains, take elevators to the nearest floor, and cut off gas lines.

Some scientists have questioned whether the programs like Japan's are worth the expense. (As of 2008, Tokai was still waiting for its "big one.") Robert J. Geller, a U.S. geologist at the University of Tokyo, has suggested that earthquake prediction might actually be impossible.

Detecting Earthquakes with Sound

Researchers at Scripps Institution of Oceanography in San Diego, California, announced in 2006 that they had developed a way of using ultrasound imaging to get a picture of an earthquake while it is still developing. They bounce high-frequency sound waves off objects and analyze the pattern of their echoes. This is the same way medical ultrasound imagers work. Bouncing ultrasound is also used by bats to find their prey and also in underwater sonar systems that ships use to navigate. But in this case, the sound waves are sent through the ground.

Knowing how fast ultrasound waves travel through Earth's crust and the time it takes the echoes to return, computers can calculate the distance from the machine to each object. By mapping vibrations in the ground, they can figure out exactly where an earthquake started and how large it was. The ultrasound system gets results within ten to twenty minutes. This information is especially valuable for predicting tsunamis, the powerful sea waves set off by large undersea earthquakes, while there is still enough time to save lives.

There are just too many factors involved, many of which cannot be measured. It is likely that scientists will keep on trying to develop prediction methods, however. There is too much at stake in terms of lives and property that could be saved by reliable forecasts.

Finding better ways to predict volcanic eruptions seems urgent as well. A really big one could do an enormous amount of damage. Scientists have found evidence that some gigantic volcanic eruptions—at least twenty times as large as the 1980 eruption of Mount Saint Helens—occurred in the past. In fact, one of them, in Siberia around 250 million years ago, may have had a devastating effect on life on Earth. It spewed out about 400,000 cubic miles (1.7 million cu. km) of lava (320 times as large as the Mount Saint Helens eruption). About the same time, according to the fossil evidence, up to 95 percent of all the marine species became extinct. Changes in climate due to the huge amounts of particles the eruption sent into the atmosphere may have been what killed them.

If a huge volcanic eruption occurred in the near future, it could have a devastating effect on the world's human population. An eruption at Yellowstone, for example, could drop up to an inch (3 cm) of ash on places as far away as New York City, Boston,

This illustration shows the smoke and ash plume that would move over North America if a giant volcano erupted in Yellowstone National Park.

and Montreal. The ash would black out television, radio, and telephone signals. Collapsing power lines and clogged generators would shut down electric power systems, and volcanic dust in the air would stall the engines of jet planes. From geological evidence, we know that the last major eruption at Yellowstone occurred about 600,000 years ago, and the two before that at intervals of 800,000 and 600,000 years apart. So we could be due for another "big one" anytime.

Where's the Quake?

The U.S. Geological Survey has online maps that show the locations of the latest earthquakes in the world. At http://earthquake.usgs.gov/eqcenter/recenteqsww/, you can click on a world map to find out about earthquakes that have occurred in the last hour, day, or week. Californians worried about getting caught in "the next big one" can go to http://earthquake.usgs.gov/eqcenter/step/ to see the probability of strong shaking in any location in that state. The color-coded map, updated every hour, is based on historical earthquake patterns. The calculations also consider information on any recent quakes and the behavior of aftershocks. After a big earthquake, this website can help people in the area to be better prepared.

Never-Ending Power Source

The magma that lies beneath Earth's crust is a huge potential source of energy. Scientists use the term *geothermal energy* for the heat energy that comes from inside our planet. In some parts of the world, it is easy to tap into the energy stored in the magma, because it comes close to the surface. In such places as Iceland and Japan, the water from hot springs is used to heat homes and other buildings. This is not a new idea. The ancient Romans had bathhouses that were heated by nearby hot springs. Modern technology, however, has made it possible to use the geothermal energy of magma deep beneath Earth's surface, as well. It not only heats buildings but can also be used to produce electricity. Power stations pump cold water through pipes that go down to the hot rocks in magma beneath Earth's crust. As the water hits the rocks, it turns into steam.

Geothermal vents—hot springs—in Iceland produce heat and electricity for home and industry. They also provide residents with a warm lake to swim in.

The steam shoots back up through pipes to the power station. The force of the rising steam is strong enough to turn giant wheels called turbines. The turbines change the energy into electricity.

Most of the world's electricity comes from burning oil and coal. But these energy resources are limited. They could be gone in just a few centuries. And burning them causes a lot of pollution, which

Why Do People Live Near Volcanoes?

Volcanoes can be dangerous. But living and working near them can also have some benefits. These include:

- New volcanoes are a great place to grow crops. Lava and ash are rich in minerals from deep inside Earth. After an eruption, these minerals eventually get into the soil. For example, Java, an island in Indonesia, is one of the world's top rice growers. These farming areas are located around volcanoes.

- They are a great place for mining precious minerals such as gold, copper, silver, lead, zinc, and diamonds. These minerals have cooked within the magma deep inside the planet for thousands or millions of years. Volcanic eruptions carry them to the surface.

is bad for the environment. Geothermal energy is a renewable energy resource. That means it can be made by the planet over and over.

More than twenty countries around the world, including the United States, Italy, New Zealand, and Iceland, use geothermal energy. In the United States, millions of households already use geothermal energy. This number is growing each year, as people are looking for pollution-free energy sources.

Plate Tectonics on Other Worlds

Is Earth the only planet in our solar system with tectonic plates? Observations made by spacecraft suggest that volcanoes probably played an important role on the Moon and Mercury at one time. However, both the Moon and Mercury are much smaller than Earth and lost their internal heat more rapidly. Their volcanoes have been inactive for the last billion years.

The dark features on the bottom left of this image of the Moon are lava-filled regions on the surface.

Did You Know?

The man in the Moon—the features of the "face" that people see in the Moon when it is almost full—is actually made up of volcanic craters and dark flows of lava.

The *Pioneer Venus* spacecraft measured high concentrations of sulfur in the atmosphere of Venus in 1979. Over the next few years, these concentrations decreased. This may be an indication that a huge volcanic eruption had occurred around the time of the flyby. Radar images of Venus sent back by the *Magellan* spacecraft beginning in 1990 showed volcanoes and also long, curving valleys similar to the oceanic trenches on our planet.

Until recently, scientists believed that Mars did not have tectonic plates. In 2005, however, the NASA *Mars Global Surveyor* spacecraft finished mapping the planet's magnetic field. Analyzing the maps, researchers found signs of transform faults, suggesting that Mars has tectonic plates similar to those of Earth. The magnetic maps also showed a pattern of stripes that typically forms when two divergent plates are pushed apart by magma flowing up from the mantle. So Mars apparently has areas where new crust is being formed, similar to the seafloor spreading on Earth's Mid-Atlantic Ridge. It was already known that Mars has volcanoes, although they all seem to be extinct. Olympus Mons on Mars is the largest volcano in the solar system. A cone-shaped mountain 18 miles (29 km) high and 372 miles (600 km) wide, it may have

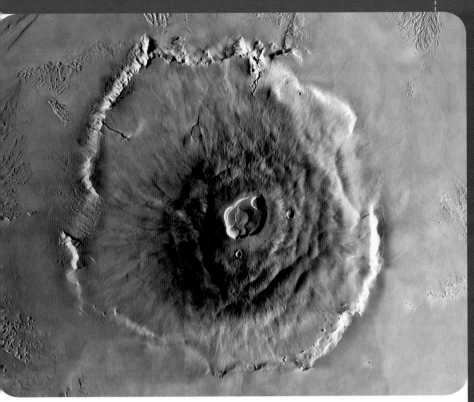

This image taken from a space orbiter shows the largest volcano in the solar system—Olympus Mons on Mars.

continued to erupt for a billion years. The discovery that Mars has plate tectonics explains its volcanic activity, as well as some other features of the planet's crust. The Tharsis volcanoes, for example, lie in a straight line. They may be the result of movement of a tectonic plate over a hotspot in the mantle below, just as the Hawaiian Islands on Earth were formed. The Valles Marineris canyon on Mars looks like it was formed by two tectonic plates pulling apart. This huge canyon is six times as long and eight times as deep as the Grand Canyon in the United States. Stripes in the map of Mars's magnetic field correspond to the Valles Marineris canyon.

Jupiter's moon Io is the most volcanically active body in the solar system. The black, gray, and red regions all show recent volcanic activity on Io.

Signs of volcanic activity and tectonic processes have also been observed on three of Jupiter's moons—Europa, Io, and Ganymede—and on moons of Saturn, Uranus, and Neptune as well.

Volcanic eruptions allow some of a planet's internal heat to be released, and this heat is radiated out into space. This is a slow but continuing process on our dynamic Earth. Eventually, like the Moon and Mercury, Earth will have lost so much of its internal heat that convection in the mantle will stop. And so will the tectonic processes that shape and reshape our planet's surface. But scientists have calculated that billions of years will pass before that happens. In the meantime, the pattern of continents and oceans will continue to shift and change, affecting the lives of all Earth's creatures.

Glossary

active volcano: a volcano that is currently erupting or has recently erupted

aftershocks: tremors (usually small) that follow a large earthquake

ash: the semisolid portion of the mantle beneath the lithosphere

asthenosphere: the hot, semisolid upper layer of the mantle

basalt: a type of rock consisting of dark-colored lava

body waves: fast-moving seismic waves that spread through the planet

caldera: a large bowl-shaped crater formed when an empty magma chamber collapses or the top of a volcano is blown off during a violent eruption

cinder-cone volcano: a cone-shaped volcano mountain formed by repeated eruptions in which cinders and ash build up close to the vent

cinders: lava broken into particles and containing many gas bubbles

composite volcano: a cone-shaped volcano formed by alternating layers of lava and ash; also known as stratovolcano

continental drift: the theory that Earth's continents have slowly moved apart after splitting off from a single supercontinent, Pangaea

continents: the large landmasses of Earth

convection currents: circulation due to the upward movement of the heated portions of a gas or a liquid

convergent boundaries: boundaries between tectonic plates that are moving toward one another

core: the innermost part of the planet

crater: a bowl-shaped hollow at the top of a volcano that forms when matter is lost during an eruption

creep: slow, steady movement of tectonic plates at a transform boundary

crust: the outermost (surface) layer of the planet

divergent boundaries: boundaries between tectonic plates that are moving apart

dormant volcano: a volcano that appears inactive but is capable of erupting

earthquake: trembling or shaking of the ground due to vibrations in Earth's crust caused by sudden movements of tectonic plates

earthquake belt: an area of frequent earthquake activity

epicenter: the spot on the surface directly above an earthquake's focus

eruption: a sudden, violent outburst; the ejection of molten rock, steam, or other matter from a volcano or geyser

extinct volcano: a volcano that last erupted a long time in the past and is not considered capable of erupting again

fault: a break in a body of rock; the boundary between moving tectonic plates

flood eruption: the release of thin, runny lava that can spread out over great distances

focus: the place where rocks break or move, producing an earthquake

foreshocks: minor tremors that occur before a large earthquake

fossils: preserved remains of ancient life

friction: the resistance to movement of two moving surfaces rubbing against each other, or the rubbing of two moving surfaces in contact, generating heat

geologist: a scientist who studies Earth, its composition, and processes of movement

geothermal energy: heat energy from inside Earth

geyser: a hot spring that sends up fountainlike jets of water and steam into the air

Gondwanaland: the southern supercontinent believed to have existed in the past

hotspots: regions in which magma seeps through weak spots in Earth's crust

hydrothermal vents: gaps in the ocean floor that erupt superheated water

lapilli: tiny pieces of rock ejected from an erupting volcano; it means "little stones"

Laurasia: the northern supercontinent believed to have existed in the past

lava: the melted rock that comes out of an erupting volcano, or the rock formed when it becomes solid

lava bombs: rocks formed by softened lava that fall close to the vent

lithosphere: the outermost layer of the planet, consisting of the crust and the upper part of the underlying mantle; it is composed of tectonic plates

magma: hot, melted rock beneath or within Earth's crust

magma chamber: a giant pool of molten rock (magma) beneath Earth's surface

mantle: the layer of the planet between the crust and the core

marsupials: primitive mammals whose young are born at a very immature stage and complete their development in a pouch on the mother's abdomen. Most of the world's marsupials live in Australia.

meteorologist: a scientist who studies weather and climate

mid-ocean ridge: a region in which a group of volcanoes forms along the ocean floor

Modified Mercalli scale: a system for measuring earthquakes' effects

Pangaea: a large supercontinent into which all the landmasses of Earth are believed to have been joined about 300 million years ago

placental mammals: mammals whose young develop inside the mother's uterus and are nourished from her blood through an organ called the placenta

plate tectonic theory: the theory that Earth's crust is made up of movable plates of rock

P waves (primary waves): the fastest body waves, which stretch and compress the rock in Earth's crust

pyroclastic flow: a mixture of lava and hot gases that may flow rapidly down a volcanic mountain after an eruption

rhyolite: a type of rock consisting of light-colored lava

Richter scale: a system for measuring earthquakes' power, or magnitude

rift: a canyon or valley, especially the gap along the middle of mid-ocean ranges

seafloor spreading: the formation of new ocean bottom where two tectonic plates are moving apart

seismic waves: vibrations transmitted through the ground during an earthquake

seismograph: an instrument that measures the vibrations transmitted through the ground during an earthquake

seismologist: a scientist who detects, measures, and studies earthquakes

shield volcano: a volcano with the shape of a low, broad dome, formed by repeated flows of lava

subduction: a process at the boundary of two colliding tectonic plates in which one plate draws down or overrides the other

surface waves: slower-moving seismic waves that spread along Earth's surface

S waves (secondary waves): slower body waves that produce a shearing movement, up and down or sideways, perpendicular to the direction of the P waves

tectonic plates: the large pieces of rock that make up Earth's crust

tiltmeter: a device that can detect tiny ground movements

transform boundary: boundary between tectonic plates that are sliding past one another

trench: a long, narrow channel in the seafloor, where subduction occurs

tsunami: an unusually large ocean wave produced by an earthquake or undersea volcanic eruption

vent: the opening in a volcano from which lava erupts

volcanic dust: lava broken into very fine particles

volcano: an opening in Earth's crust through which hot matter escapes from the mantle below; or the cone-shaped mountain formed around the opening by the buildup of lava and ash

Selected Bibliography

ABC. "Magnetic Field Maps Mars's Tectonic Plates." *ABC News*. October 18, 2005. http://www.abc.net.au/news/stories/2005/10/18/1484641. htm (October 3, 2008).

Aylesworth, Thomas G. *Moving Continents: Our Changing Earth*. Springfield, NJ: Enslow, 1990.

Ballard, Robert W., and Walter Cronkite. *Exploring Our Living Planet*. Washington, DC: National Geographic Society, 1994.

Bowler, Sue. "Recycling the Earth." *New Scientist*, January 17, 1998, 1–4.

Browne, Malcolm W. "Experts Ponder Causes of Breakup of Ancient Supercontinent." *New York Times*, October 3, 1995, C1, C9.

Farndon, John. *How the Earth Works*. Pleasantville, NY: Reader's Digest Association, 1992.

Hui, Li, and Jeffrey Mervis. "China's Campaign to Predict Quakes." *Science*, September 13, 1996, 1,484–1,486.

IBS Communications. "The Destruction of Pompeii, 79 A.D." *Eyewitness to History*. 1999. http://www.eyewitnesstohistory.com/pompeii.htm (September 30, 2008).

Kious, W. Jacquelyne, and Robert I. Tilling. *This Dynamic Earth: The Story of Plate Tectonics*. Washington, DC: U.S. Geological Survey. 1996. Online edition. March 27, 2007. http://pubs.usgs.gov/gip/dynamic/dynamic.html (October 7, 2008).

NASA. "Advanced Technologies." *Innovation*, September/October 1994. http://ipp.nasa.gov/innovation/Innovation25/DanteII.html (October 2, 2008).

Pinter, Nicholas, and Mark T. Brandon. "How Erosion Builds Mountains." *Scientific American*, April 1997, 74–79.

Pollack, Andrew. "Japan Questions Its Costly Program to Predict Earthquakes." *New York Times*, January 13, 1998, F4.

Science Daily. "Fire under Arctic Ice: Volcanoes Have Been Blowing Their Tops in the Deep Ocean." June 26, 2008. http://www.sciencedaily.com/releases/2008/06/080625140649.htm (June 26, 2008).

———. "Forecasting Aftershocks: U.S.G.S., Caltech Seismologists Develop Online Tool to Predict Aftershocks." September 1, 2005. http://www.sciencedaily.com/videos/2005/0905-forecasting_aftershocks.htm (October 29, 2008).

———. "Real-Time Quake Detection: Seismologists Use Ultrasounds to Assess Quakes Faster." April 1, 2006. http://www.sciencedaily.com/videos/2006/0406-realtime_quake_detection.htm (September 30, 2008).

Time-Life. *Planet Earth*. Alexandria, VA: Time-Life Books, 1997.

Topinka, Lyn. "Mount St. Helens, Washington Regrowth and Recovery Images 1980–Current." *U.S. Geological Survey.* December 4, 2006. http://vulcan.wr.usgs.gov/Volcanoes/MSH/Images/recovery.html (October 8, 2008).

———. "Mount St. Helens Returns to Slumber." *U.S. Geological Society.* July 10, 2008. http://vulcan.wr.usgs.gov/Volcanoes/MSH/Eruption04/Monitoring/July2008/ (August 14, 2008).

UNESCO. "Surtsey." *World Heritage.* July 8, 2008. http://whc.unesco.org/en/list/1267 (August 15, 2008).

USGS. "Mount St. Helens—From the 1980 Eruption to 2000." *U.S. Geological Survey.* March 2000. http://pubs.usgs.gov/fs/2000/fs036-00/ (October 7, 2008).

Wiley, John P., Jr. "Mapping the Margins." *Smithsonian*, April 1997, 68.

Williams, Martyn. "Japan Activates Earthquake Warning System." *PC World*, October 1, 2007. http://www.pcworld.com/article/137878/japan_activates_earthquake_warning_system.html (October 3, 2008).

For Further Information

Books

Green, Jen. *Mount St. Helens*. Strongsville, OH: Gareth Stevens Publishing, 2007.

Johnson, Rebecca L. *Plate Tectonics*. Minneapolis: Twenty-First Century Books, 2006.

Rooney, Anne. *Earthquakes and Volcanoes*. San Diego: Silver Dolphin, 2006.

Rubin, Ken. *Volcanoes & Earthquakes*. New York: Simon & Schuster Children's Publishing, 2007.

Steele, Philip, and Neil Morris. *Inside Earthquakes*. Strongsville, OH: Gareth Stevens Publishing, 2006.

———. *Inside Volcanoes*. Strongsville, OH: Gareth Stevens Publishing, 2006.

Stewart, Melissa. *Earthquakes and Volcanoes FYI*. New York: HarperCollins, 2008.

Vogt, Gregory L. *Earth's Core and Mantle: Heavy Metal, Moving Rock*. Minneapolis: Twenty-First Century Books, 2007.

———. *The Lithosphere: Earth's Crust*. Minneapolis: Twenty-First Century Books, 2007.

Watt, Fiona. *Earthquakes & Volcanoes*. London: Usborne Books, 2007.

Woods, Michael, and Mary Woods. *Earthquakes*. Minneapolis: Lerner Publications Company, 2007.

———. *Volcanoes*. Minneapolis: Lerner Publications Company, 2007.

Websites

Dive to an Active Submarine Volcano
   http://www.pmel.noaa.gov/vents/nemo/dive.html
   This interactive website lets kids ride a remote-controlled vehicle to the seafloor and back.

The Earth Inside Out

> http://www.kidsgeo.com/geology-for-kids/
> 0037-the-earth-earth-inside-out.php
> This site has a simple introduction to Earth's structure,
> plate tectonics, and volcanoes, illustrated with great color
> photos and diagrams.

Earth Like a Puzzle

> http://www.sio.ucsd.edu/voyager/earth_puzzle/
> A kid-friendly site on how the theories of plate tectonics
> and continental drift were developed, with interactive
> activities to work with your mouse.

Earthquakes, Volcanoes, and Plate Tectonics

> http://sciencespot.net/Pages/kdzethsci2.html
> This site has links to kid-friendly educational sites from
> the U.S. Geological Survey; the Franklin Institute; PBS,
> "Savage Earth"; TheTech (online museum exhibits on
> Earthquakes); FEMA for Kids; NOVA, "Deadly Shadow
> of Vesuvius", and lots more.

Earthquakes for Kids

> http://earthquake.usgs.gov/learning/kids//
> On this site, find out what earthquakes have occurred in
> the past week, past month, and important earthquakes
> in history. Other pages include Cool Earthquake Facts,
> Earthquake Pictures, Science of Earthquakes, Science
> Fair Project Ideas, Puzzles and Games, and Become an
> Earthquake Scientist.

Plate Tectonics

> http://science.nationalgeographic.com/science/earth/
> the-dynamic-earth/plate-tectonics-article.html
> Find articles from *National Geographic* on plate tectonics
> and earthquakes ("The Next Big One" and "Wrath of the
> Gods") on this site. It also has a video, a photo gallery, and
> links to the latest Earth news stories.

Pompeii: The Last Day
http://kids.discovery.com/games/pompeii/pompeii.html
Learn about volcanoes and build your own virtual erupting volcano in
VolcanoExplorer on this site. Kids can also follow the Pompeii story
in text, pictures, and videos and take a quiz to see if they would have
survived the eruption.

Index

About the Authors

Dr. Alvin Silverstein is a former professor of Biology and director of the Physician Assistant Program at the College of Staten Island of the City University of New York. Virginia B. Silverstein is a translator of Russian scientific literature.

The Silversteins' collaboration began with a biochemical research project at the University of Pennsylvania. Since then they have produced six children and more than two hundred published books that have received high acclaim for their clear, timely, and authoritative coverage of science and health topics.

Laura Silverstein Nunn, a graduate of Kean College, began helping with the research for her parents' books while she was in high school. Since joining the writing team, she has coauthored more than eighty books.

Photo Acknowledgments

The images in this book are used with the permission of: © Mary Evans Picture Library/The Image Works, p. 5; © The British Library/HIP/The Image Works, p. 6; © Kristian Dowling/Getty Images, p. 7; © Romeo Gacad/AFP/Getty Images, p. 8; © Laura Westlund/Independent Picture Service, pp. 10, 12, 19, 20, 22, 25, 28, 35, 38, 56, 81, 85; © David McNew/Newsmakers/Getty Images, p. 13; © Ken Lucas/Visuals Unlimited/Getty Images, p. 15; © Bildarchiv Preussischer Kulturbesitz/Art Resource, NY, p. 18; © Marli Miller/Visuals Unlimited, Inc., p. 23; © Bernhard Edmaier/Photo Researchers, Inc., p. 27; OAR/National Undersea Research Program (NURP)/NOAA, p. 29; © Pegasus/Visuals Unlimited, Inc., p. 31; Integrated Ocean Drilling Program, p. 33; © Arctic-Images/Iconica/Getty Images, p. 37; Submarine Ring of Fire 2006 Exploration, NOAA Vents Program, p. 39; © Julian Hibbard/Photonica/Getty Images, p. 40; NASA, pp. 41, 105, 107, 108; © age fotostock/SuperStock, pp. 42, 45, 47, 49 (top), 61, 79; © SuperStock, Inc./SuperStock, pp. 44 (left), 66; © iStockphoto.com/John Carnemolla, p. 44 (right); © Fred Kamphues/SuperStock, p. 49 (bottom); AP Photo/Courtesy USGS Cascade Volcano Observatory, Harry Glicken, p. 51 (top); © Photodisc/Getty Images, pp. 51 (bottom left), 52; © Jim Sugar/CORBIS, p. 51 (bottom right); © Martin Gray/National Geographic/Getty Images, p. 55; © ARCTIC IMAGES/Alamy, p. 59; © Donna and Steve O'Meara/SuperStock, p. 60; © Kaj R. Svensson/Photo Researchers, Inc., p. 62 (left); © Charles Schafer/SuperStock, p. 62 (right); © DEA/C.DANI-I.JESKE/De Agostini Picture Library/Getty Images, p. 63; © Science Source/Photo Researchers, Inc., pp. 65, 67 (bottom); © Purestock/Getty Images, p. 67 (top); © Joanna B. Pinneo/Aurora/Getty Images, p. 68; © Photononstop/SuperStock, p. 69; © Pacific Stock/SuperStock, p. 70; © Todd Strand/Independent Picture Service, p. 71; © Craig Mitchelldyer/Getty Images, p. 72; © Otto Greule Jr/Getty Images, p. 75 (top); © John Storey/Time & Life Pictures/Getty Images, p. 75 (bottom); © Gary Weber/AFP/Getty Images, p. 76; © American Stock/Hulton Archive/Getty Images, p. 77; U.S. Geological Survey/photo from Hebei Provinical Seismological Bureau, 1976, p. 88 (top); AP Photo/FILE/Chiaki Tsukumo, p. 88 (bottom); AP Photo/APTN, p. 90; © SSPL/The Image Works, p. 92; © Adek Berry/AFP/Getty Images, p. 93; © Peter Parks/AFP/Getty Images, p. 94; AP Photo/Koji Sasahara, FILE, p. 99; © Simon Terrey/Photo Researchers, Inc., p. 101; © Images&Stories/Alamy, p. 103.

Front Cover: © Ryan McVay/Stone/Getty Images.